ARE YOU READY YET?

PROTECTING AND PREPARING YOUR FAMILY FOR ESTATE ISSUES BEFORE AND AFTER DEATH

ARE YOU READY YET?

PROTECTING AND PREPARING YOUR FAMILY FOR ESTATE ISSUES BEFORE AND AFTER DEATH

Michael C. Wittenberg CFP® certificant,
AIF®, ChFC®, REBC®, CWS®, CLU®, RHU®, CRCP™, PPC®

Library of Congress Control Number:		2019909957
ISBN:	Hardcover	978-1-7960-4706-6
	Softcover	978-1-7960-4707-3
	eBook	978-1-7960-4708-0

Printed in the United States of America.

Rev. date: 08/13/2019

To order additional copies of this book, contact:
Xlibris
1-888-795-4274
www.Xlibris.com
Orders@Xlibris.com
798955

To my family, my clients, and all caregivers.

Certified Financial Planner® certificant
Accredited Investment Fiduciary®
Chartered Financial Consultant®
Registered Employee Benefits Consultant®
Certified Wealth Strategist®
Chartered Life Underwriter®
Registered Health Underwriter®
Certified Regualtory and Compliance Professional™
Professional Plan Consultant®

CONTENTS

Orientation

My name is Michael Wittenberg, and I will serve as your guide on life's journey from wellness to illness, to death, as well as with estate issues after death has occurred. My goal is to help you prepare for the inevitable for yourself and those you love. My approach is practical and concise, offering you action steps along with an understanding of how and why those possible actions may benefit you. I will show you the location of planning "land mines" and how to avoid them.

As I write this, I am privileged to continue serving wonderful individuals and families as their financial adviser. Since I am in the thirty-sixth year of my career, unfortunately, I have seen many good people succumb to illness and death. Many individuals wisely realize the truth of the adage, "Health is wealth."

Across our nation, some families are better prepared, and others are unprepared. Whatever degree of preparation you have made, whether any at all, and wherever you or a loved one is on life's journey, these ideas will serve you as valuable tools.

Like other professionals, I have developed a viewpoint based on my studies, work, and life experiences; and based on what I have found to be valuable for clients, I will make understandable the reasons why I have reached my conclusions. However, you could reach quite different views. You may not value what I value. A pitfall into which professionals can easily fall is interweaving their values into their work for you without disclosure, presuming you share them.

Consider this book as a providing you with a baseline or a starting point to further inform you. There are lots of food for thought, along with many prudent steps for you to consider, that help you and those you love. I hope this book motivates you to become better prepared so you can protect yourself and your family.

Atypical for an investment professional, I earned a master of science in mental health counseling degree. I tease that this degree is essential for working with the vagaries of stock markets. Additionally, I have a graduate degree in education, and as of this writing, I hold nine certifications in my field.

I teach at a renowned community college that has been visited by two US presidents—George W. Bush and Barack H. Obama. I joke that they both heard about the five classes I teach on Medicare, social security, retirement, investments, and estate planning. My college teaching career began in 1986; I kid that I started teaching when I was nine years old.

This work is my practical memoir written to help you. Let's dive in; the water's warm.

Avoid Starting Your Journey "Left of Foot"

Do you want to dramatically increase your effectiveness in guiding professionals on how to best serve you?

For a moment, suspend looking at yourself from the vantage point of a client, and look at yourself through the eyes of the professionals who assist you. Let's pull aside the curtain and go backstage. You may have never considered this before, but the professional you sought out may meet several new clients each week or even each business day. How do you metaphorically embed in the mind of that advisor a glowingly positive view of you? How do you stand out as an impressive individual, couple, or family whom the professional looks forward to serving and getting to know well?

Alternatively, do you leave the pro and their team with the impression you could be challenging to serve? Said differently, have you ever considered how you behave and what you radiate as a customer, client, or patient? Do you overgenerously grade your behavior as a client on a steep curve, or would you be happy to have your behavior interacting with your attorney's paralegal erred, captured on a smartphone for the nation to see? Do your professional service providers see you similarly as you see yourself in the role as a client? Did you ever ask them how you can work better with them and what you could do differently to help them serve you more effectively?

"Michael, I pay the professional, and their fees are expensive. So that should be more than enough." Do not all the professional's active clients pay their invoices or find themselves quickly becoming former clients? How do you ignite their passion for metaphorically going through walls to help you because you stand out positively as likable? "That's not my job, Michael. A professional is supposed to bring it." Agreed. Still, do you want to be one among many, or do you want to shine? Haven't you, at times, been reinforced sometimes by the gift of the smallest kindness, maybe just one thoughtful remark that inspired you to want to climb mountains beyond your professional duties for someone when you were not required to go that extra distance?

"Wait, Michael, I expected this book to explain what relevant professionals will do for my family and me." This work will do that and much more. However, just as any client is a person first and a client second, the same applies to any professional. Do you like everyone at work, in your church, in your neighborhood, or even in your family? Pros decide whom they care about more. Your behavior, demeanor, and attitude influence how the adviser and their supporting teammates see you and whether they treat you above and beyond.

Appropriately, you will be assessing whether you want a given professional serving on your team. Simultaneously, the professional and their team are evaluating whether they think that there is "goodness of fit" between you and them. After the meeting concludes, it's not a unidirectional decision to work together.

Some clients bring the check. Meanwhile, other clients bring politeness, pleasantness, respect, and gratitude along with their check for payment. Isn't that also what you'd like the professional and their team to deliver and reflect to you as they provide you the service you seek?

Once when I was joking with a medical professional, attempting to make their hectic day just a tad bit more enjoyable, she told me, "Michael, all of us like you." This response led me to ask, "If you don't mind sharing, as I work with clients, how do you handle a patient who routinely behaves in an ornery fashion?" She said, "We do everything we are supposed to do for them. We do not do anything less than we are required, but we don't do anything more than required for them."

I didn't write this to do an "O woe is me" for any professional. They selected and remained in their career, so they own the positives and negatives that come with their job, no different than your position or role delivered to you. This work isn't about the professional's requirements or preferences; this book is about your needs. Hopefully, you are mostly a great client, customer, and patient. I want you to consider, Is that accurate or not? Would you, if you were the professional you seek out, want to serve you as a client? How much extra, if you were the pro or their team, would you want to do for you as a client?

If you are not already an exceptional client, what, if anything, are you and your family going to do differently to help align all the service stars on your team in your favor? It takes just a tiny bit of thoughtfulness on your part to stand out. You can motivate a professional and their team to give you every possible benefit, far beyond the standards of their profession.

Plan to Plan

A small amount of time planning for the first meeting can make it far more productive as well as comfortable for you and for whomever you bring with you (such as your spouse or your adult child), ultimately yielding you outsized results. What I urge my students to do, whenever possible, is to write down what is essential for the upcoming meeting. What is most critical for you to convey to that professional and their team? Many people are familiar with this idea, yet so few individuals do this.

Are you going to see your longtime physician? At a minimum, write down what has changed regarding your health since your last visit and every question you wish to have answered. In the scrum of discussion, it is possible to forget to mention something important to you. Please write it down. Have a copy to hand your physician. Review it while you're in the waiting room as your review may trigger an additional issue. Some physicians refer to verbose patients disparagingly as "He's a talker." They see the patient as a "time sink" who provides the physician with no additional clarity regarding their medical condition, just wasting the doc's precious time.

Time is the most critical resource a professional (or anyone) has. Actively help them by utilizing the time you need, but no more. Do you have a hectic schedule? In those free moments while waiting amid some errand, at least type your questions and concerns into the notes section of your phone.

Suppose you decide you are going to set an appointment with an estate planning attorney highly recommended by someone whom you know to be savvy in the ways of the world and whom you trust. In this hypothetical, let's say not only will this be the first time you have met this attorney but also you have never met with an attorney for estate planning purposes. Let's further stipulate in this vignette that you do not think you know much about the area of expertise of the professional with whom you plan to meet.

Call the office of that professional to inquire if the initial consult is complimentary. Today, many professionals, particularly attorneys, tax and investment professionals, do not charge for the initial consult. If it does cost, ask if it is a flat fee or if "the meter is running" and, if so, at what hourly rate.

Also ask, "How long does the adviser allot for the first meeting?" For example, my team books me for ninety minutes for an initial meeting. If there is a specific amount of meeting time known to you in advance, you can mentally set aside the last fifteen minutes of your session for some concluding or closing questions that will help make your meeting even more successful.

When initially calling, have your and your guest's preferred day and time but also an alternative ready to request. It is courteous to let the consultant's staff know the name and relationship of your guest.

Having two predetermined preferred dates makes scheduling easier for you, while your organization may wow the pro's teammate responsible for scheduling. With the staff and the adviser, you only get one chance to make a first impression, and that's bidirectional as they only have one opportunity to make a pleasing, professional first impression on you.

What action steps do you take beforehand to become well prepared so you will have a productive meeting? It is vital that your keyboard type or that you handwrite legibly, necessary for identifying information. I refer to this handout for the professional as your distributed summary. Retain your copy as your preferred meeting road map. Create two additional copies of your distributed summary. You will give one copy to your prospective adviser. You will have already provided your second copy to your guest. After your mutual introductions and pleasantries, present a copy to the professional, explaining what you have done and asking them to please take a moment it to read it to aid and guide the meeting.

While the pro is reading, make no comments. If you speak while the adviser is reading, they may miss something due to your distraction that neither you nor the professional may realize. If you wisely brought someone else with you, don't speak to them while the pro is reading your distributed summary. To me, multitasking means doing two or more tasks at the same time poorly.

You can profitably use the silence to review the second list of questions (or comments) that you have also prepared before the meeting, which I refer to as your retained question list. This second list is not something you choose to give to the professional. If your meeting veers away from what you prefer discussing, your second list helps you quickly regain control of the direction of the meeting to achieve your aims. The main goal of your retained question list is to enable you to be fully prepared to ask thoughtful questions that help you elicit the core information that you want to receive from the professional.

Successful meetings occur when individuals, couples, and families use the allotted meeting time to discuss what is most salient to them, helping the professional clearly understand what they seek. However, often, both the prospective clients and the professional may spend too much time gathering necessary information, wasting valuable meeting time and sometimes leaving the client feeling rushed and not fully heard.

Similarly, the adviser must "get their bearings" of who you are, what you need, and how they may go about solving the problem you are asking them to help you address. Getting the consultant's and your gyroscopes aligned steals time from the heart of the meeting. Has that ever happened to you? If so, how satisfied did you feel about your appointment afterward if you felt rushed or not fully heard?

Number each separate item on your distributed summary for easy reference by everyone. What are some questions that may be on your summary? Step into the shoes of the pro and their staff. What general information about yourself do you think is potentially helpful, especially at the beginning of that first meeting, for that consultant's work for you? This summary will differ based on which professional you are meeting and what needs you want to convey. Below the title of distributed summary, list the following:

1. Day, date, and time of the meeting.
2. Your name and, if married or partnered, the name of your spouse (and if partnered, you state that next to their name).
3. Age of each and DOB.
4. Names, ages, and marital (or partnered) status of adult children.
5. Your profession and name of your employer. If retired, list that and the number of years retired.
6. Anything else that is pertinent for the professional to know about you and the situation that you deem so essential that you want to state it before indicating the central purpose of the meeting. Any details that are useful but not as critical, you can list after the main thrust of your mission.
7. "Meeting purpose: _____." Be concise and clear. Think of what you write as if you were the professional serving you and your family. The purposes are nearly infinite as each person, family, and situation are unique. For example, you may say, "I seek your guidance on what legal documents I need to best protect myself and family in case of disability or premature death." "I have been told that I have stage 4 cancer, and I want to consider treatment options, their remission rates, and my potential quality of life due to side effects versus palliative care." "I am in the process of a divorce. However, as we have children together, I want to be sure that my children receive my estate when I die. How can I best make this happen?" "I am remarrying, and my new spouse is much younger. I want her to have our home to live in during the remainder of her life. However, I want my children, not her children from a previous marriage, to receive our home after my new spouse dies. How do I achieve my objective?"

8. "Please explain the major steps in the process to achieve my goals and what the reasonably achievable time line is." (Or regarding process duration, said differently, "So that I understand the time parameters, what is the likely expected amount of time it will take to complete this process and achieve my goals? Quickest? Slowest?")

9. "What are the challenges or difficulties I will likely face during this process?"

10. "From your experience, what are the areas that are the most burdensome to clients who have a similar goal as me or us?"

11. "What do clients do that make your work more difficult and produce suboptimum outcomes?" (Can you imagine the surprise that the professional will have when you are asking about possible self-defeating client behaviors you want to avoid? The adviser will be impressed with your self-awareness and your desire to help the pro give you the best outcome.)

12. You accurately need to understand what the professional will charge you. Here are possible cost questions: "Do you have an hourly fee, or do you have a flat fee per type of documents, such as for a will or a revocable living trust?" If an attorney tells you that they charge a flat fee to prepare each document type, to prevent misunderstanding, ask, "As we communicate via email, phone, or additionally, in office meetings, are those communications part of the flat fee or are there additional costs involved?" "Do you require a retainer, and if so, what is the dollar amount? Will you present me with a service agreement that we both sign?" If you are required to sign a service agreement, typically, it will be sent to you after the meeting. Often, service agreements are brief. However, if you find any portion of the deal that you do not understand, email or call the professional to be sure you understand it thoroughly before signing it. Typically, it will include a thirty-day billing cycle. If the professional does not receive a payment within thirty days, you will be charged interest, often at 18 percent

per annum. These credit card–type rates of interest mount up quickly.

13. Then list either additional headings if applicable, such as "Concerns: _____." This section may be for a particularly thorny situation you or your family are facing, for example, "This is a second marriage, and my children from the first marriage and I are currently estranged." "I previously used an estate planning attorney whom I found difficult to understand due to the technical nature of his explanations." "My father has cognitive impairment and is becoming agitated more frequently." "My siblings have been disinterested in helping me care for our mother, and I am at a loss how to best handle this situation." List all your major areas of concern.

Clients may wade timidly into topics painful to them as they are revealing personal situations that they feel paint a less-than-flattering portrait of themselves or their family. Believing that their problems are so rare heightens their reluctance to act to improve their situation or that of those they love. In effect, they suffer in silence, immobilized, as if trapped in amber. Feelings of embarrassment, shame, and being less than make it excruciatingly painful for them to share some vital details.

Compounding this situation, when an individual, couple, or family finally seeks the assistance of a professional, they may be unwilling to be entirely forthcoming. Though self-defeating, it is not uncommon that clients leave out vital details or are purposely inaccurate to maintain their self-esteem and lessen their unpleasant emotions. If you only tell your physician half of your symptoms, at best, you will receive a half-correct diagnosis and plan of treatment. Once, a woman told me, "I treat my investment adviser like my gynecologist." I was wondering where this remark was heading until she wisely said, "I tell him everything." Brava!

Though they may loathe their unwanted circumstances, clients mistakenly believe their situation is so exceptional and that the professional will have never heard of such complications and may judge them harshly. Clients often do not realize that experienced professionals have listened to many variations on the same theme.

It is essential for the adviser to reassure the client that the gist of their concerns is seen quite often and is not, as the client thinks, encapsulated by some pejorative, such as "odd," "weird," or "bizarre." This reassurance by the adviser is referred to as the professional "normalizing" the client's experience. Normalizing helps the client and their loved one realize that they are not alone facing this problem. Many other people may face similar challenges, some of whom have even worse factors with which they contend. When an adviser skillfully normalizes the client's sensitive issues, the pro performs an excellent service for the client(s). The relief clients feel when they realize that they are not alone is palpable.

Mental health counselors realize that everyone is entitled to their feelings. Counselors are not in the judgment business; they are in a helping profession. Fields like law, tax planning, investments, and insurance are not typically defined as "helping professions" as are medicine, nursing, physical therapy, and counseling, for example. However, attorneys, tax advisers, and insurance, investment, and estate planning professionals can create significant positive improvements in the lives of a family, potentially helping several generations.

In my view, true professionals don't judge their clients. If you think that's occurring, it is vital to address it, asking the adviser to discontinue that behavior. Pros seek to provide solutions. A true professional is not going to bring their personal opinions into the issue. If they do, you can call them on it by saying something like, "I am concerned that your comment reflects negatively on me or my situation. How will you avoid having your personal opinions limit your ability to serve me [or us] successfully?" Think of it as a statement that's in the category of "In case of emergency, break glass." Though prepared, it's unlikely that you will need that phrase.

Like all of us, you have your style and comfort level when in a meeting. Honor yourself by not sticking rigidly to the phrases I offer above if the suggested phrasing smacks of "That's just not me." The questions provided are not sacred. You may need to rewrite the phrases in a way that sounds natural to you. If they seem inauthentic or too stilted, you are less likely to use them well. Having a host of questions that you can customize for you or your loved one's needs helps you prepare well and allows you to feel more in control.

For example, some readers may choose not to have questions 8 through 11 listed on the distributed summary, which is for the professional. They may instead prefer to keep some or all four items on their retained question list from which they use to guide the meeting and delve deeper.

When trying to grasp dimensions or magnitude of anything, you may find it useful to think of what you wish to measure as being along a spectrum or scale on a one-to-ten range, with one being the lowest and ten being the highest. Is an ill spouse or parent in pain? To understand its magnitude, you may ask, "Place your pain on a scale of 1 to 10, Dad, with 10 being the worst pain. How would you rank your pain now?"

Using this scaling tool, you may ask your loved one's surgeon, "On a scale that ranges from the lowest being one to the highest being ten, how great is the surgical risk for my [spouse, mother, father]." Alternately, ask, "How difficult is this procedure for you to perform on that scale?"

When attempting to understand the amount of your cost to pay for this adviser's services, it may be useful to ask, "I am trying to understand the possible range of costs. Besides indicating the expected cost of your services, can you also tell me what may be the range of the price from lowest to highest?"

If the answer you receive is too amorphous, it is essential to express your concern over any aspect of what you would be charged that sounds vague to you. Many times, a professional doesn't know the cost until they see the details of the work you request. However, it may be helpful to include in your distributed summary a request next to cost: "When you have completed your analysis of this task, please update me by email as to any changes in cost you then expect."

The advantage of being more prepared is that you can feel confident and equal to the adviser, so you are guiding the meeting rather than experiencing the professional's standard presentation. The reassurance you may feel from having specific comments or responses at the ready allows you to avoid coming to the table feeling you are in a "one down" position to the adviser. You are not in a "one down" position, but I do see some individuals who appear to feel that way, which is unfortunate and unnecessary. Try not to surrender your power to any professional since they work for your benefit.

I have people say frequently, "Michael, I don't know anything about your field." I respond, "Similarly, I have limited knowledge of your area of expertise. You probably know more about my field than I know about your occupation. You are successful at what you do, showing that you can become acclimated and knowledgeable regarding investing to the extent of your interest and time available." This approach helps the client reclaim their power and control in the meeting. Many individuals indicated they hadn't thought of it that way.

I want the person or couple to be at the table as an equal (that is how I want you to feel when working with any professional). They may not know my world, but they know what they want. They are more expert on themselves than any professional can ever be.

It's critical for the consultant to help the client get at the core of the client's agenda. Client organization and honesty make this possible. You want to receive the outcome you seek and are paying for to the extent feasible.

If you don't think the professional may need some information for your meeting, don't include it, or put that information near the end, before your contact info. You don't need to write a book; you want to get the adviser to focus on the heart of your issue. Less is more. To that point, Abraham Lincoln once sent a message to a friend: "I wrote you a long letter since I did not have time to write you a short one."

One style is to put your contact information at the end. Though important, the adviser doesn't typically need contact information at the beginning of the summary document that you have created.

Putting that contact info or anything general but not immediately pertinent can distract the advisor from your agenda. Remember, this summary is something you choose to create. Someone on the professional's team is going to input your contact information. Some consultants have a team member to sit in to help gather information about crucial points elicited by the adviser during the meeting for celerity and accuracy.

"Michael, at my physician's office, at each visit, I have to go over my basic information when I check in to let the staff know I have arrived for my appointment. I feel like I have signed twenty HIPAA release forms. I essentially start over reviewing my data at each appointment as if I had never been a patient there before." Then skip that info on the summary sheet you will hand to the physician, getting to the core of your concerns sooner.

Your distributed summary clarifies what is vital to you while making you more concise to help the adviser give you what you want. As you hand the consultant your summary (typically two to three pages), you start your meeting being more organized, savvy, helpful, and memorable in a most positive way.

Your job is to be explainer-in-chief of your situation and what you need to do for yourself or those whom you love. Then aim to be an especially careful listener. If you spend too much time writing, you can bog down the meeting's flow. Unless the discussion is highly technical, during the session, only take the notes that you deem essential. Possibly, your guest could capture the most critical ideas. Your distributed summary helps you succeed succinctly, allowing you to focus on what the professional is saying. This session is an interactive conversation that requires your full engagement.

You have a dual focus if you are meeting an adviser for the first time, discussing the content, the particulars of your situation, the "Here's what brought me to you today." However, you have the added task of accessing the style of the professional. Do you think from the pro's ability (or inability) to communicate, without jargon, you will like working with this adviser?

The more session time spent on discussing concerns vital to you rather than on orienting the administration, the better a feel for the consultant you will likely develop. Some terrific scientists have an uninspiring bedside manner, but some physicians offer their patients both. You are trying to figure out which of those two archetypes you have sitting in front of you in that white lab coat. Discern, then decide, if you are satisfied or not based on your impressions.

Your contact info includes your physical address as well as your mailing address if those differ, your preferred phone number, and your alternate phone numbers. Indicate if you permit the leaving of voice mail and texts on the phone numbers you provide. List your preferred email address. For some situations, it is beneficial to create a new dedicated email address for yourself so you keep the communication between you and the professional's staff organized. If that seems wise to you, have that done before your initial meeting.

Indicate their phone numbers and email addresses of those family members and friends helping you. List their names and the contact information of the professionals who are already part of your team. This team may include your attorney, tax adviser, investment and insurance adviser, medical personnel, or realtor. It is not uncommon for the professional you are meeting to have had other mutual clients in the past, with some of the professionals you have listed on your distributed summary, especially if your community is small.

You can add to your retained question list a question whether the professional you are meeting with has prior experience working with some of the professionals on your team. Does the professional you are meeting with have a good working relationship with them? Typically, if the consultant knows or has worked with some of the professionals on your team, they will tell you that even before you have a chance to ask.

Will you or someone you love serve as team coordinator or captain of your team of professionals? Alternatively, do you prefer one of your professionals to function as the team leader or a "first among equals" for the various pros who serve you? Would it remove a burden off your or your family's shoulders?

Weigh out for you and your family the advantages or disadvantages of assigning a professional to become the playing captain on your team, assuming they will accept it. High cost? May that slow the process down? Added complexity? If after your prior deliberation you want to explore the possibility of using that approach with one of your advisers, list that toward the bottom of the retained question list as you are discussing "next steps."

There is one potentially significant problem with asking one of your pros to shepherd the other professionals you utilize. It is vital to write down, either at the end of your distributed summary or in a follow-up memo, your expectations of the responsibilities of the captain of your team of professionals. If this role is poorly defined, it can lead to mutual disappointment for both you and the professional whom you ask to be the first among equals.

I am mentioning this idea for your consideration not because I am a fan but instead to show you a possible route if you and those you love are overwhelmed or so unfamiliar with the challenges you face that a professional leading may serve you better. I most prefer, when possible, a loving, trusted family member being the coordinator-in-chief if they are available, up to the task, and willing.

This is crucial: if you are primarily reliant on a family member or other professional who has your most profound trust, convey that person's name, title, and role to all your advisers. Furthermore, who is the real decision maker, you or someone else? Also, please be sure to list on your distributed summary the contact info of family if you have made someone (or been made by someone) an agent of a durable financial power of attorney and a health-care POA.

What my clients and I have found most useful is someone serving as the communicator among the professionals (think horizontal communication) and between the advisers and the family (think vertical communication). Being conscientious about the prompt transmission of information to various team members, for example, via an email shared with all your professionals, is vital. Consider encrypting the update for confidentiality. Decide who will undertake the communicator task. Will they send out a weekly update each Friday or only on an ad hoc basis?

The communicator begins by conveying their plan for updates, such as frequency and timing, which helps everyone, professionals and family alike, know what to expect. Date the messages in bold and large font. You may wish to refer to the number of the updates as each summary is an edition, as a periodical. Try to create a standard format so that all the readers can quickly find what is most relevant to them.

Add to your distributed summary whatever you face that is significant to you that the professional needs to know so that they are fully informed. If it is salient to you, the pro must know.

Run your summary through a software for grammar and punctuation so that your distributed summary is equal to the professionalism you expect to receive from your adviser. Then you are ready to colead a successful meeting.

Think about how much you will "wow" the professional you seek to serve you if you adopt some of the suggestions above. The adviser will respect your effort. Your organization and well-considered summary, as well as your incisive questions, will signal to them, "With this client, I have to keep on my toes, and I want to deliver my best work for them."

You win!

The Center of the Bull's-Eye

Suppose you are now in a meeting. When any professional recommends a course of action to you, softly ask something along the lines of, "So that I am sure I understand your advice, please review the reasons for your recommendations." Utilizing that phrasing, you are politely asking your attorney, tax or investment adviser, physician, architect, or another adviser one question: why? "Why should I follow your advice?" "How does your advice serve my loved ones and me?" Write this type of question on your retained question list. Phrase it your way so your words are natural to you. However, don't try to recall it; please write it down. If you need to, during the meeting, read it from your retained question list.

In some instances, when you are using the word *why*, it could be taken as you being rude. "Why did you do [or think] that?" implies criticism of their action. Often, the person moves from listener to defender, raising their shield into a sturdy defensive posture. This word usually cuts off the open, relaxed sharing needed for robust candid communication. The word choice using *why* seems like a challenge, possibly that a negative, even derisive, judgment is looming. The stakes of the discussion seem to get higher. While you are merely trying to understand, to be sure the advice offered fits you well, the listener may hear you are calling them to account, as if their recommendation is somehow deficient.

Here's a useful variant, though it's turned up just a notch: "I want to be sure that I am not misunderstanding. Help me review how your recommendation achieves my goals, consistent with my values." This sounds more formal, maybe even stiff, but you score points. When in doubt, ask, "What is the reason . . ." which is the same as asking why but without any bite to it.

Then move on to what's also vital: "Let's review the potential pitfalls that I may face if I follow through as you recommend." If you choose to follow the advisor's plan, it is critical that you understand the risks you undertake. Can you accept the implications of a possible unwanted outcome? If not, what alternatives acceptable to you do the professionals have to offer?

Please be aware of the amount of meeting time remaining. At no later than fifteen minutes left, ask the professional for just a moment to look at your notes. Then take these two steps. First, you say to the advisor, by looking at your retained question list where you have your preferred phrasing—what is natural in style to you—written verbatim for your comfort and ease, something like, "Now that we are finishing up, I'd like to restate what I understood from this meeting." Give your verbal summary of what you discerned. Your restatement lets the pro correct anything you may not fully understand. This review helps both of you have a mutually similar sense of the vital points discussed during the meeting.

Then second, go to "What are the next steps you and your team will take, and what next steps do you expect me and my [family, spouse, parent, or child] to take?"

If your initial impressions from this meeting are positive and you think it is likely you will want to continue working with the professional, consider a phrase or two that you believe would show you to be gracious and classy as your meeting concludes.

You did it! Great meeting!

No Mind Reading

Please let your adviser and their supporting teammates know your preferences. "You cannot reach me in the morning, but after lunch works with my typical work schedule." "I am a teacher. I cannot even go to the bathroom during the workday, let alone receive a call. I prefer an email, and then I will call you after 3:15 p.m." However, ask to whom the professional prefers that you give that "My Preferences" information, which you can include at the end of your distributed summary.

Often, it's a team member keeping track of the details for the adviser who needs that type of information, not the adviser. Frequently, a staffer is reminding the consultant about your preferences as they structure the activities of the adviser to honor your preferences, sometimes without the awareness of the professional.

Don't be reluctant to state your preferences; after all, you are the paying client. However, be willing to inquire if what you seek is "in bounds or out of bounds" for the service work of that profession. Those who fail to ask typically don't get. Many times, the requests are so reasonable that the team is delighted to accommodate you as it gives them a concrete way for them to shine for you.

Once while I was at my allergist's office in an exam room, as his nurse exited, she accidentally left the door ajar a sliver. I could hear my physician softly call out to her, "What room? What room?" He needed to know which patient is next. He wisely did not try to serve as his own traffic cop, and in fairness, his patients were seen "first come, first served."

Since you are the client, at times, support staff may not wish to tell you a polite version of "No, we are not able to meet your preferences." In a perfect world, they would immediately be candid, but the professionals outrank them. A team member may have to run your request by the professional after you have left the office. Watch for the staffer's unspoken no.

Yes, you want what you want, but if you come across as inflexible, you may be defined as potentially tricky to please from the get-go. A wise adviser listens carefully to the "read" of their staff regarding the behavior and demeanor of new clients, some of which appear out of the sight of the professional. If the team cannot do what you consider to be essential, you need to continue your search. The old saw about working with an attorney is that there are two rules: you must be able to pay their fee, and if you are not willing to take their advice, then find another attorney.

Meeting "After Action"

The meeting is over. You've left. Find a nearby coffee shop to write down any essential information you do not want to forget. Put the date and time on your postmeeting notes.

If you chose to bring a relative or friend to the meeting, first, process their experience of the meeting before sharing your thoughts about the session and the professional. It is critical to review their understanding of the information and write notes while they are telling you their takeaway from the meeting. Then you can move from content to what their sense of the professional and his or her staff was.

When you canvass your relative, though it is difficult to avoid, it is essential not to let their perceptions influence your takeaway from the meeting. Your understanding and theirs may be the same in many respects but not all. The following questions are for both yourself and your guest, who may be a spouse, adult child, parent, or close friend. What do you think of the meeting's content? How did you think about and feel about the professional during the conference? How would you rate the meeting and the professional on a one-to-ten scale with one being low and ten being high? Ultimately, your impression of the conference is what matters most. Your relative or another guest may offer confirming or disconfirming data and opinions, but it's your viewpoint that's critical.

Ask your family member to do the rating and have them offer you their results first. They may ask you simultaneously, "What did you think?" Please indicate that you wish to avoid influencing their perception of the meeting, so you are purposely going to debrief them first, then you will be happy to share your takeaways after gathering their opinions, which will further enhance the discussion.

Your meeting guest's scoring of the meeting and the professional could be quite different from yours, and ironically, it could say little about either the pro or the session. Either or both of you could offer quite different scaling results because some individuals tend to be very critical raters, thus grading low on many evaluations, while other raters customarily rate products, services, or personnel with high marks. Their scaling of the meeting and the professional may not "say much" about either but may instead be more telling about the rater's yardstick.

You will have to decide what you think the validity of their assessment is. Do you consider your guest's views as being on point and savvy? If you believe that there's little value to their takeaway, what is the reason you asked them to join you for the meeting? Sometimes, the answer is, "They are the only family member available. For my comfort, bringing someone is better than going to the meeting alone." It could also be, "I am not focused as much on their perceptions. Rather, I asked them to join me to help me capture the factual content." "I wanted to feel less stressed and less anxious, so I invited them because I find their presence reassuring."

Please consider, before the meeting, the weight or reliance that you want to place on opinions of your meeting guest, keeping in mind their human limitations. Will your meeting guest be impacted at all by the decisions you make and the work of the pro? Alternatively, are they there primarily to buttress your meeting efforts? Remember this sage advice: only give limited credence to your guest's assessments unless they experience the same impact as you. If they do not suffer the consequences, only you will, then their opinion, no matter how wise, needs to be given only its due and nothing more.

Also remember, your unconscious and subconscious knows way before your conscious mind knows. Listen to the message you are receiving from your body on a gut level. I refer to this as trust your instincts but don't leave your reasoning skills and intelligence outside in the parking lot. Were your goals for the session achieved? In effect, were the main concerns you had addressed? Finally, were you pleased, and did you come away liking, trusting, and being impressed by the knowledge of the professional? Do you want to employ them to serve you?

Retain your copy of your distributed summary. Store that in your digital or paper file related to the work of this professional and their team. Also, store any notes you made during the meeting as well as your "after action" records. Memorializing the process may later help refresh your memory. Let's say the task baton is being passed to another family member undertaking the work. If unfortunately incapacitating illness or death has occurred, notes can be priceless as milestones on the road you wanted to travel for yourself and those whom you love.

Your purpose is not to become a scribe or stenographer; however, I have seen clients uncertain what to do at the time of their parent's death because Mom or Dad didn't tell them of their preferences or left few records. Even a few notes can make all the difference for a family trying to reconstruct and understand the process that previously unfolded and what you or your loved one wanted.

Some professionals will give you a summary paragraph of their understanding of the discussion at the meeting's end, and some will mail you a postmeeting summary. Some will do neither. You can ask as part of your "What are the next steps?" question, Will the professional or a staffer send you a postmeeting wrap-up note or not? If appropriate, when do we meet next?

If you choose to send the adviser a brief note as your takeaway from the meeting, include (a) expression of gratitude for their time and insights; (b) what you understood as the core of the meeting, especially any decisions; and (c) what steps you will take and what steps you understand the pro and their team will undertake. Be concise. Keep a copy of your meeting follow-up letter in your file. If you are pleased to work with them and that you are happy that this work will be tackled, sounding positive and upbeat serves as encouragement to the pro and their team.

Manners Win

This chapter is the last of this work focused on your interactions with your team of professionals and their team members. When dealing with the office of professionals, please do not make this mistake; do not be rude to staff, even when they err. Some educated individuals behave in an unbelievably rude manner. If you think such behavior is uncommon, I wish you were correct. Unfortunately, it is not so.

For you, sometimes, your greatest ally is a subordinate of the adviser to whom the pro delegates enormous discretion. You need a request fulfilled. Sometimes, the staff will make it happen or choose not to without the involvement or awareness of the adviser. Sorry, someone on the team, at times, will not have gotten or will have forgotten "the memo" regarding a given service preference that you requested. Politely remind them, accent on being polite, as opposed to expressing annoyance with staff. If chiding staff helped you in the long run, I would recommend it, but it doesn't. You may momentarily feel better if you vent; however, you probably will sink your ship. Diplomacy is much more likely to serve you better.

The professional's team members are not your employees. Certain rights you may ascribe to yourself as a client you may not legitimately have. Unless egregious, it is often best if you request of staff that they address their mistake, allowing the team the opportunity to rectify it. Any subsequent error, you are calling your consultant. When speaking to your adviser, please do so in an unemotional manner, sticking to the facts as you experienced them. After that, talk to the consultant's supervisor. No resolution will likely lead you elsewhere.

When you think of staff, remember we need all the friends in life we can make. There is usually one or more staff upon whom the pro heavily relies. Often, the team does the bulk of client service work, not the adviser. The adviser employs their skill, but most of the day, their team members are entrusted to make significant decisions in running the machine that is the office. The adviser's team delivers much of your client experience, not the adviser.

Make friends with the staff generally but figure out who is the professional's "right arm." The consultant forms a sense about you while you're in front of them; that positive or negative impression is either reinforced or altered by your behavior with their team.

Some clients are verbally aggressive, even mean, to staff, while they are simultaneously polite to the professional, sometimes during the same phone call. It's known in the corporate world as "kiss up and kick down." A wise professional will defend their staff and may drop you as a client if you feel entitled to be rude to their team members.

Please start by offering the benefit of the doubt that you may be misunderstanding a rule, requirement, or procedure that affects the professional, their staff, or all clients. If upon explanation you come to understand it was you who erred and not the team, please acknowledge it. That's primarily for your benefit, not theirs, as you will be showing your classiness. If you approach your concern without certainty, as making an inquiry rather than immediately launching into a tirade based on self-certainty, you will be more respected. You wisely didn't accept being treated like a doormat. However, you also didn't presume you were correct because "That's not how the bank does it" when you are at an investment firm, not a bank.

When dealing with anyone, you have two choices. When there's been a bump-up, do you want to be triumphantly correct? Alternatively, do you want to maintain and strengthen the relationship while fixing the problem? Clients (spouses, other family members, and friends) get angry when they feel *hurt*. Anger can also reflect feelings of *anxiousness*. Do you sense that the person feels distressed and anxious? If you can keep that in mind when dealing with your spouse, children, parents, coworkers, direct reports, supervisors, and your advisers and their teammates, this will help you immensely. If you assuage their hurt feelings instead of defensively snapping back, addressing or ascertaining what may be causing their anxiousness, their anger may subside. They may apologize to you.

It's not easy to have such presence of mind or to keep calm when you are on the receiving end of someone's anger. In the department of easier said than done, if you can treat their anger as not being about you but rather about how they may be feeling disrespected and anxious, arguments can melt away. In a sense, your expressed concern about their feelings disarms the aggressive party as you attempt to discern *what's underlying their anger, hurt, fear, and anxiety.* If you stay at the level of symptoms, the fight continues ("You didn't take the trash out"). When the angry party has a moment to reflect, in their eyes, your IQ went up twenty-five points, and your niceness quotient reached the chart's zenith.

Recall some past service error of which you were on the receiving end. Does this seem accurate to you? The customer, client, or patient is angry less at the perceived or real error than at the lack of caring they intuit they are receiving as evidenced by the failure. Some clients see it that if the professional and their team truly respected them, the team wouldn't have made such a mistake. Frequently, it is how the client defines what the error betokens or says about them or the team's view of them, which may have triggered their emotion.

Some errors "scream" to customers and clients, "You don't care about me. You are treating me like a number. I don't matter." It feels like a betrayal, an abandonment, and a hypocrisy, especially after the professional and their service team stated how terrific the client's service experience would be.

Do you treat the adviser and staff as innocent until proven guilty or immediately as guilty as charged? You do not even have to say words to that effect, but the team picks up which approach you are taking. Clients, staff, and professionals leak how they feel.

Please do not misinterpret this as allowing errors to go uncorrected. I am not lobbying you to accept the unacceptable. Pick your issues, and do not make them battles. Explain dispassionately while being open to the possibility that what seems like an error to you may not be. Don't try to kill a mosquito-sized irritant or mistake with a nuke since it won't help you or your loved ones get your needs met in the future. Do you want to win? Be classy.

Bringing a box of doughnuts as you arrive, completely unexpected and unnecessary, which costs you little, makes you stand out as such a thoughtful, caring person. The team likely wants to go out of its way to reciprocate, not because of the doughnuts per se but because you went above their routine experience. You showed your interest and respect, which is what you want from them.

As a client, customer, and patient, you will err, as will the professional and their staff, unfortunately. Three incredibly potent words are "Please forgive me." I have yet to meet any client, staffer, or professional who didn't respect and accept a sincere apology.

When a company makes an error, the term for the response by the company to fix the error is *recovery*. Business professors have thoroughly studied this topic. If what the company's employees do to rectify the error is seen by the customer as an excellent "recovery," the customer becomes *more loyal* to that business *than they were before the error occurred!*

You may have been so impressed with a given company's recovery response that you shared your experience in complimentary remarks to family, friends, and coworkers. They made an error that negatively impacted you, and now you love them! Not only is it what the company did but also, in their recovery effort, they worked to treat you respectfully. They restored to you your "face," your self-concept as an individual deserving respect; you felt their recovery was fully rectifying.

Let's apply the concept of a first-class recovery to you. Even if you currently have weak relationships with some of your service providers, decide which of those relationships you will retain and which you prefer to end. Since you do not control the service provider's behavior, only your response, what will you do to try to turn the situation around with those you will continue to use to meet your needs so you receive a better service experience?

"I'm The Boss! I Do Not Want Ever to Die!"

In the next chapter, we'll begin examining wills and trusts, which tie to action steps. Before we get there, let's tackle several major conceptual topics that intersect now. This chapter intertwines fear of loss of control and fear of death—the ultimate loss of control—as well as authority and responsibility. As an example, we will explore an ordinary though critical situation that families face: when someone they love may no longer be driving safely.

Sometimes I hear, "My children are telling me what to do, Michael! I was wiping their behinds before they could walk. They think they know better and are going to tell me! No way!" Please be candid with yourself (or be frank in your assessment of the loved one you are helping). Is your situation or personality such that you must maintain control, or will you be comfortable with delegating some authority to family members and professionals?

Whether about family or work issues, it is vital that the authority given to the individual must be commensurate with the responsibility entrusted to the individual. It is not uncommon that the responsibility thrust upon a given party is far higher than the authority granted, leading to, for example, the frustrated family (and in the world of work, frustrated employees and supervisors, both of whom may have so much responsibility and insufficient authority to meet their obligations adequately).

If you are helping someone as a caregiver or if someone is helping you, have you given or have you received authority equal to the responsibility you are charged with or have undertaken for your loved one? If the answer is no, then consider your first task is to bring up this topic to the individual who has the authority, some of which you need to receive to complete your responsibilities successfully. If you are the recipient of care, please consider what you have asked your loved ones to do for you and if you are holding their reins so tightly it makes their efforts to aid you much more onerous. Are you helping them help you, or are you impairing their ability to help you?

If you are feeling like the handcuffed caregiver, it may be structurally impossible for you to excel at caregiving. Having a frank, though gentle, conversation along the lines of, "I so much want to help you, Mom. However, I feel that I am seeming inadequate as I cannot readily achieve what you are asking me to do. I feel disappointed and hurt that you are choosing not to allow me to make decisions that need to be made promptly for tasks that you asked me to do for you. Then I feel as if my efforts are displeasing. I respect if that is not your intent. However, that's what it appears and feels like to me. How can we fix this so we are both satisfied and so that my authority is equal to the tasks you want me to complete for you?" Think in terms of changes you would like to see made that are constructive; be ready with your suggested improvements.

As a caregiver, it may take a while for you to receive authority commensurate with the responsibilities you agreed to take on. Making progress toward that positive end is difficult unless you recognize the gap between the two and have discussed it with your loved ones.

Let's move back a step to see how the need for control fits into estate planning broadly into preparation for severe illness and death. Why is it often delayed? Estate planning is delayed sometimes because of its cost or when the individual or family does not know where to begin. Sometimes, estate planning is postponed because the individual does not want to think about death or do the organizational work involved, or they do not yet feel comfortable creating a plan of action to delegate to others, be they professionals or family.

Delegating, relinquishing, and graciously accepting the loss of control can prove most difficult for many individuals to do. Generally, we love our autonomy and do not like anyone to attempt to circumscribe our control over our own lives. I see that as an inherent, firmly held human attribute or preference. However, I find some individuals resist relinquishing control at all costs, sometimes to their detriment and to the exasperation of those who love and are trying to assist them. In other cases, I see the ill or aging family member delighted to be able to stop doing specific tasks and gladly surrendering some responsibilities with feelings of relief.

For adult children assisting a parent, it may be helpful to consider the following. I have not met anyone who did not enjoy their independence of decision-making, finances, mobility, and timing, that is, being able to choose what and when they wanted to do it.

If you are an adult child, you may be at the height of your powers—worldly, decisive, skilled, and successful. Many times, for aging parents, that is not what they are experiencing. That's part of their past, and their illnesses or other infirmities are nagging, even hurtful, reminders of their sliding quality of life, which can feel so scary and sad to them. They may feel uncomfortable that they are losing control. For many, their decline signifies that unwanted death is creeping closer. I have met individuals terrified about death, frightened even thinking about it, while others don't want its arrival yet accept it is as natural as birth. It is difficult to understand the magnitude of the impact that fear of death has on some people. It is debilitating.

Fear of death inhibits otherwise highly intelligent people from acting in their own best interest or the best interest of their loved ones. At nearly all costs, some people avoid facing, discussing, and preparing for the inevitability of death. They can run as fast and as far as possible. And while they have no difficulty intellectually understanding that death always eventually wins the race, however, emotionally, they avoid accepting, at all costs, that they are likely to face severe illness and then die. Sometimes, those costs are so high for themselves, their spouse, and other family members whom they love so dearly. Though different for each of us, there are specific mirrors into which we all are afraid to gaze.

I am not criticizing this most human behavior; I do wish it wasn't so since it is self-defeating. However, it exists, and it is not uncommon. I love the quote from Roman antiquity by Terence, who wrote, "I am human, and nothing human is foreign to me." You may not agree with the behaviors of others. When you strive to understand them from their viewpoint and how or why they believe those behaviors serve them (even when their responses prove self-injurious), often they will appreciate your effort. A lack of understanding may block empathy and compassion; however, knowing the reasons for the actions of those you love does not signify your approval of certain self-defeating behaviors. Knowledge and understanding are not the same as giving a license to or condoning those behaviors.

If you are the caregiver, if possible and appropriate, ask the individual you are assisting questions tied to their emotions. What are their hopes about their current predicament? What are they most frightened will happen? Sit with those ideas patiently, and do not tidy them up by whisking them away with palaver. "I want to understand how you feel, brother. Help me get a sense of what it would feel like for me to be you." In the face of severe disease and the approach of death, sometimes our words are inadequate. Our presence and our silent support, our listening, along with some well-considered heartfelt words, may be the only tools we have available at a given moment. They may be just what your loved one needs at that moment.

Probably the most used defense mechanism of most humans as uncovered by skillful researchers in the field of psychology is avoidance. Probably better than 90 percent of the time, using the defense mechanism of avoidance leads to failure, additional problems, and stress. In short, avoidance most often does not work well, yet for most humans, it is a well-worn rut. Talking to those you love about what feelings they may have that could be inducing their avoidance may help them and you. "What are your greatest fears over your upcoming surgery?" As you listen, it is crucial that you do not dismiss their fears with soothing words like "It will turn out well," which the individual may receive as you negating the validity of their feelings of worry.

What is it you most want to convey? "I'd love to get beneath discussing the superficial and ask you to share with me, if you wish, what you are thinking and feeling about all this? If you don't prefer to do that, please know I am happy to listen if you, later, want to have a discussion."

Let's dive deeper. From studying human development, social scientists have learned that at about age fifty, individuals start the process of more seriously contemplating their mortality. After fifty, there is a tendency to consider our eventual death more frequently. The notable exception for this is if a young family member or a contemporary die prematurely. This shocking, and seemingly nonnatural, reversal of their expected life span often triggers an early exploration of one's mortality.

For example, I have witnessed no suffering among my clients greater than a loss of their child. Its pain is incalculable. I had seen it well to the surface in an instant as if the loss of their child occurred yesterday when the child died five decades earlier.

I so dislike the term *closure*. There are some griefs so deep that there is no closure. In the face of some pain, I see that term as an unintended insult by those who don't "get it." When feeling uncomfortable in the face of someone else's indescribable pain, they think they need to have something to say that sounds intelligent to still their anxiousness. I see that as a vacuous, unhelpful term at best. Please refrain from pronouncing *closure* for someone else. The only people who can use that term with legitimacy, in my view, are those suffering the loss.

If you are in the bloom of health and success, consider how you may feel if you knew your powers were failing due to serious illness or aging. Please think how hard it may be for you to truly understand, despite your immense love for a spouse, parent, or others whom you love, how hurtful surrendering their autonomy feels. It may sting them so bitterly that they resist acknowledging the need to relinquish some aspect of their independence indefinitely. I see so many individuals fight to maintain maximum autonomy if they can even when doing so is no longer helping them.

Many times, driving is the flash point for an intergenerational battle. "Michael, I no longer drive on the highway, and I only drive nearby to the grocery store, and I go after 10:00 a.m. when everyone is already at work so the roads are uncrowded." Though I admire their efforts at risk mitigation, they either are capable of driving safely or they are not.

When I was wisely alerted that my mom seemed unsteady as a driver, I approached her with, "If we agree to take you anywhere you want to go so that you retain full mobility, would it be okay if you discontinue driving so that we know that you will be safe?" Thankfully, I received an affirmative answer, and my mom never drove again.

The issue that sometimes is incendiary is when adult children fear that the driving ability of a parent has deteriorated to such a degree that the parent is a danger to themselves, their passengers, pedestrians, and other drivers. What I have found useful is to arrange an alternate travel system, and now that ridesharing vehicles have become ubiquitous, this is easier for the adult child to organize for their parent while being cost-effective.

Some older adults work to remain computer savvy. However, if your parent has been unwilling to venture beyond a flip phone, they may need to call you or whoever has set up a ridesharing account for their use when they need transport. The caregiver then can request the vehicle to pick up Mom or Dad for the grocery, medical appointments, hair salon, and other short trips. It is helpful when the adult visits their parent on a day off from work to accompany Mom or Dad on their errands using the ridesharing or taxi service. This experience may acclimate your loved one to this alternate means of travel, making the process familiar and undaunting.

Many towns offer free transport for those with severe medical conditions, who are older, and who have limited financial means on a scheduled pickup basis to the physician's office, for example. Also, various charitable organizations have a network of volunteer drivers who will take a person in need of individual appointments. In larger towns, there are more services available for older and ill residents are.

See if one of the social service agencies has someone who could help you navigate the resources for yourself or a parent or other relative. Sometimes, the hardest part is finding out about available resources, though often they are discovered by the impacted individual themselves conversing with friends or neighbors who are somewhat similar in age or medical condition.

When being honest with yourself or if you ask your loved one to be candid with themselves, are you or they finding it difficult surrendering control? Ask, "What may help to make it less painful?"

To generate less resistance, gently approaching the discussion may succeed. Rather than making a courtroom case filled with what you consider to be airtight evidence as to why a spouse or mom or dad should refrain from driving or about any other activity or responsibility, try to stay at the level of how they may feel. Being fact-based may backfire as they will likely come back with their "facts" to disprove or discount your thesis.

If factually their driving ability is not sound and they resist your recommendation to discontinue driving, you can call the DMV and explain your concerns. DMV may choose to have them come back in for a road test, or they can have someone (either from the DMV or local police) observe your parent's driving, and they may have their license revoked if your concerns are warranted.

Please note, if not handled well, this approach could lead to a rift if your loved one learns or intuits that you were involved behind the scenes, resulting in their loss of driving privileges. That's the advantage of the police following them intentionally and making a professional determination as your fingerprints are nowhere near the scene of your effort to safeguard your implacably resisting loved one. You do the right thing in love for your resistant, unrealistic parent while valuing and attempting to preserve your relationship with them.

Referring to my comment above, approaching this softly or gingerly, you may have more success in your discussion if you ask and not tell. Ask how your spouse, parent, or other loved one feels about the issue. "How safe do you feel as you drive? How may we help you?" Then listen without judgment (challenging for you or anyone to do, I agree).

Verbally reflect what you have heard. "Mom, I am hearing you saying . . ." This phrase allows your loved one to amplify their remarks, to correct anything that you misheard or they didn't initially explain well.

It may help if you remain at the level of feelings. "Dad, I love you so much, and I feel worried about your well-being as well as the safety of your passengers, pedestrians, and the safety of other drivers. If you would like, we could brainstorm a plan where you will be able to maintain full control over when and where you go without needing to drive any longer. I would gladly take this burden off you. I know you would never want to hurt anyone else, especially someone you love. I want to help you be able to travel whenever you need to, and I have some ideas on how we can make this work well for you."

Sometimes, focusing on the needs of the three other constituencies, such as their spouse or other passengers, pedestrians, or other drivers, helps them see that it may not be useful for them to only focus on their desire to drive. If you can assist your loved one in meeting the needs that they obtain from driving, this may help them see their needs achieved by other means, which may eventually prove reassuring.

If your loved one were initially skeptical, that would be understandable. You and they may benefit if you underscore that if the first attempts do not work, there are other alternatives that you both can try until they have smooth access to reach their destinations.

When you ask them if you may hold their keys if you think that's wise, be sure to get all the spare sets too. I have seen family initially want to sell their parent's vehicles to use the proceeds for their care, only to be stopped by their parent under the guise of "When I get better, I will be able to drive again." The adult children may tell me, "Michael, my dad will never drive again."

However, the adult child may refrain from selling their parent's vehicle, though they retain firm possession of the auto's keys as they realize that the visible presence of the car provides their loved one with hope and motivation to become well so that one day, they may able to drive.

We all need whatever we view as tasty carrots dangling up ahead motivating us to move forward. Instilling hope is one of the greatest gifts one person can give to another. It may be even for a small achievement; however, having hope is priceless in its ability to motivate individuals. Bring positivity, confidence, and hope to others, and their life and yours will be happier.

There are many other issues about which you and your loved one may not see eye to eye. After listening to them, reassure them that you respect how difficult this must be for them and that you love them and want to care for them well. As much as possible, during your discussions, try to imagine if you were them and what they might be feeling. As your compassion flows, you will help them, and you may even earn their buy-in over time.

Building Blocks

There are four foundational legal documents you can use to protect yourself and those you love while living as well as after their or your death. I have yet to meet an estate planning attorney or read a publication in my field that didn't praise the protective value of the big four. These include (a) a will, (b) a durable financial power of attorney (FPOA), (c) a durable medical power of attorney (MPOA) with a HIPAA release form, and (d) an advance directive, sometimes colloquially referred to (though misnamed) as a living will. I will explain these four, each in a chapter ahead, as well as other documents mentioned below.

Sometimes, I see one or two additional documents that my clients have had their attorney draw up, the first of which has been in much more widespread use the past few decades—the revocable living trust.

A more complex document with a specific, valuable aim has two monikers. In the past, it was referred to mostly as (f) an irrevocable life insurance trust (ILIT). An ILIT now has a less jarring and more palatable marketing name as a wealth replacement trust (WRT). Attorneys still refer to this type of trust as an ILIT. Insurance agents who sell the life insurance policies used in the ILIT refer to it as a WRT.

Though I happen to have all six documents myself, that doesn't mean that having all six mentioned above is right for you or a loved one. As in all things in this book, check with an attorney knowledgeable about estate planning to see what best fits your situation and needs.

Sound advice may be expensive, but it also may prove priceless for you and your family.

I will mention some critical ideas on all six documents as we travel further together; however, as an additional reminder, my goal is to make this valuable information approachable and usable. Since I am not an attorney, I make no claim these descriptions or information are precise. I aim to help you "get" the big picture. This book is designed to help you become conversant with concepts that will enable you to understand better what your attorney may relay to you in your meetings. Your legal counsel can provide valuable legal advice and precision. This work contains neither.

While many attorneys studiously avoid this, from client reports, some attorneys unknowingly lose their clients in legalese during the meeting. That will not happen in this work. However, do not treat this work as a substitute for sound legal advice by an attorney knowledgeable about estate planning.

In addition to these six legal documents, I will explain several other mechanisms commonly used to transfer assets at death successfully. These will include beneficiary clauses and designations, which are ubiquitous, valuable, easy to use, and with which you likely have familiarity.

I'll examine the uses of free payable-on-death and transfer-on-death forms. Financial institutions use these forms to help their clients prepare to transfer assets in their accounts quickly and efficiently to their beneficiaries upon their death (though there can be catches and *they may not be the right tool to use in some cases*).

As a teacher, I have found "spiral learning" to be effective. This term refers to introducing a topic, learning a bit about it, then reintroducing it later. When reintroduced, we will take a deeper dive into that topic.

Also, at an investment or brokerage firms, two specific documents can be useful called a limited trading authorization form and its more powerful adjunct, the full trading authorization form, which I will explain in a chapter up ahead.

It is easy to imagine how it can be incorrectly assumed that everything legally necessary is the result of legislation passed by the US Congress, signed into law by a president, with the new statutes fleshed out by supporting rules developed by some federal agency. In the two vital areas this work will touch upon, each of the fifty states, not the feds, does most of the heavy lifting in insurance and estate matters. Why is this important?

You understand we, the people of the US, are incredibly mobile people. This residential mobility may reflect your personal experience. Several clients have shared with me that their career or their spouse's career led to twelve or more family moves, remaining in a new locale for only two or three years before packing up to relocate yet again and living in Alabama this year before uprooting to North Dakota next year. Today, domestic US moves sound quaint as the country shuttle is becoming more familiar with people moving from the US to countries and cities across the globe.

You may have previously moved permanently across state lines before, or you and your family are considering pulling up stakes to move permanently halfway across our beautiful country. Your career opportunities may not precipitate your move, but instead, you may relocate for retirement. As the baby boomers are accelerating their pace of saying adios to full-time careers, some are exiting states with an exceedingly high cost of living for much cheaper living elsewhere in and outside the US.

You may be planning to sell your high-market-value home, taking cash from its juicy price appreciation to purchase another home elsewhere. Visualize moving to a state with a lower cost of living, more amenities to your liking, lower state taxes, closer to family, or to return to the place you lived during your formative years that feels most like home to you. The overage—the remaining principal amount beyond your cost to purchase another residence in your new home state—is often employed to produce additional income to make retirement even sweeter. For some readers, this move is already in their rearview mirror. Congrats! I hope that your retirement proves to be the best job that you have ever had!

It could be that if you are an aging parent, you are moving closer to one of your children to have nearby support, or maybe you are an adult child moving closer to your parent to provide a watchful eye and a helping hand. You may move somewhere else, and that new locale becomes your new permanent primary residence, for example, for a decade, and then you move to the state next door or ten states away and set up a new permanent home. You lived in Maine, and while in Maine, you wisely had an attorney recommend and draw up the all the legal documents you needed for estate planning purposes.

Happily, when offered a terrific new position in sunny California, you and your family move there, and in all respects, it becomes your new home. You receive mail at your new address; you vote in local elections in your county. You pay state and local (property) taxes and do everything that you formerly did that your legal and tax adviser indicated made you a legitimate resident of the state of Maine.

Suppose I made such a move, what would I do that's critical to protect my family and myself? I would find a skilled attorney knowledgeable about estate planning and show that attorney all my current legal estate documents as well as copies of any beneficiary forms I had signed and if I added payable-on-death (POD) or transfer-on-death (TOD) beneficiary forms at a bank or an investment firm. I would ask, "Is it best to protect my family by having all new documents like those mentioned at the beginning of this chapter, or is there some reason that's not necessary?" The process of having an estate planning attorney draw up all new documents is known as repapering.

When I discuss this in class, there's the undercurrent of, "Michael, you know you will certainly be advised to repaper—to get all new legal estate documents drawn up specific to the new state of permanent residence—because it is lucrative to the law firm." I am not naive that this could occur; think caveat emptor. Ask the attorney, "What benefits do I garner if I repaper? Moreover, what possible problems can occur if I don't repaper?"

You get to decide what you prefer to do, knowing the benefits and pitfalls. Are you soon moving back permanently to the state that all your estate planning legal documents were drawn up? Tell the attorney your tentative plans. If there is a compelling reason to or not to repaper your estate legal documents, an ethical professional will give you sound advice. In an abundance of caution, I would likely repaper, but most especially if my counsel recommended it. Why? I would want to be repapered because each of the fifty states has their statutes related to wills, trusts, and probate so that everything aligns well.

Let's look at a few possibilities. Suppose you have had no legal documents drawn up for you or your spouse or that you have some documents but may need some additional estate planning documents or that you have the proper estate planning legal documents required but you created them years ago. Let's further suppose that your situation has changed, so you need to repaper to meet your current estate planning needs. We will first look at some critical issues related to a will.

"I Will! I Will! I Will!"

As we zero in on a will, what I have noticed was years ago, I might come across someone wealthy who had a twenty-five-page will. Today, some of the wills of the wealthy I have seen are a mere three pages in length. What has led to this change? During the past quarter century, revocable living trusts have become much more widely used as an estate planning tool, even among individuals with modest assets. Some attorneys, to protect clients' privacy, have moved specific information as to who receives what asset at death, typically in the deceased's will, to the revocable living trust.

Why? Wills are public documents filed at the county courthouse available for public inspection in person or via the internet. This explanation is for understanding, not precision. Consider a revocable living trust, which is a nonpublic legal document, as a contract. Typically, the only individuals who have a right to see the contents of the revocable living trust are those individuals whom the deceased chose to leave some of their assets to, as listed in the revocable living trust. Bingo! Privacy!

Other family members may be curious; however, if they are not a recipient of assets under the revocable living trust, they usually have no right to read the trust document, so they do not know who got what bequest. While there are other benefits for some individuals from the use of revocable living trusts, lack of public disclosure has been the primary driver for revocable living trusts for some of my clients. However, other benefits beyond privacy may serve a given individual well.

I have seen specific items (for example, a piece of real estates, such as a beach house), a dollar amount, or percentage of the deceased's total estate assets mentioned in a will or a revocable living trust going to a named individual. Suppose the same verbiage was used, with the heirs receiving the identical bequests, regarding privacy, what's the difference? In the case of the will, any member of the public could read the terms of the will.

Ghoulish though this may sound, some businesses "mine" or search wills for selling opportunities. Based on the assets listed in your will, what may a salesperson be able to sell to your family? The revocable living trust is not a public document, so there is no requirement to file it at the courthouse for required availability for public inspection like a will. It remains private.

What is the purpose of having your will (or that of your spouse or parents) available for anyone to read? It allows family members and likely heirs to see what the deceased set down in their will, typically as created by their attorney. If one or more family members think what they read improperly excludes them from assets of the deceased's estate, they can bring an action in probate court. This dispute is a "will contest."

A will can be set aside by probate court. While this can and does happen, it is essential to retain a proper perspective and not hyperventilate over this possibility. Most estates pass through probate court readily, without any problems, as there often is no controversy among heirs. Probate is a necessary though routine process designed to prove that the will presented is indeed the last will (the most current version of the will) of the deceased.

Our nation's post-WWII baby boom generation (1946–1964) is so numerous that our nation's average age is skewing older, with boomers retiring at the rate of ten thousand per day. The US population is living longer, which brings the unfortunate by-product of increasing numbers of individuals afflicted with various forms of cognitive impairment. If you are a caregiver, such as an adult child, it is critical that you be aware that if the will and other relevant documents are kept at your parents' home, for example, in a fireproof box, sometimes, the individual moves their records to another unique location.

Caregiving family members, as well as the executor (often the same person), may be aware of the location where their parents keep their vital legal documents. Often, the family may be unaware of the repositioning of the will and other essential documents as there is no discernible benefit for the cognitively impaired individual from the documents' movement.

The individual with cognitive impairment often fails to tell their family that they moved these critical documents. If their loved ones are fortunate enough to realize the will is no longer secure in the expected location while their parents are still living, the afflicted individual cannot recall why they moved their documents or to where they moved them. What's even worse is when the individual has died, the family goes to the fireproof box at their parents' home, only to discover no essential documents are there, which they were sure were in this safe place. This surprising and unwanted discovery starts a feverish hunt throughout the house. Crucial to note, if you find a copy of someone's will but not their actual will, that won't fly in the probate process.

At times, a family member will report to me something like this: "Michael, I have been writing out mom's checks to pay her routine monthly invoices for several years. Recently, from a few late notices, I figured out that now my mother must be failing to put the mail in our agreed location on the dining room table. When my mom was well, she paid all her bills the day they'd arrive. These late payment notices would mortify my mother. I was looking for something in the garage, and then I found wadded-up papers shoved into a crevice. That led me to look around. Then I realized that my mother is taking the invoices and other mail, even junk mail, and hiding it in other strange places throughout the house." This sad situation is not uncommon.

The will needs to be kept in a safe place. Attorneys often offer to hold on to their clients' wills, both for the safety of the client's legal documents and so that it may predispose the family of the deceased to use that attorney for estate administration and settlement issues.

If you have worked successfully with a different attorney other than the one your recently deceased loved one used, you can call the law firm, telling them you want to pick up, for example, a parent's will. They may have you sign a note confirming you retrieved it and may want to see your driver's license for identification.

Often, wills are kept in the safe-deposit box that an individual may have at the bank. While the will would be physically safe, especially in the past, this could be problematic as once the bank employees learned their customer had died, they were required to seal the safe-deposit box. Today, many institutions can remove for the benefit of the family only the will, with the rest of the contents of the lockbox still sealed. Please check at the bank what its policies are, as determined by state statutes, as far as the family being able to retrieve the will from a safe-deposit box after the individual died. It is typically less problematic if one of the spouses is still living and they are up to the task, physically and cognitively, of retrieving the will of their newly deceased spouse. Headaches can occur for the family when the parent is the last of two that dies regarding lockbox accessibility.

If you anticipate a family fight upon your death or upon the death of your last surviving parent, get thee to thy legal adviser ASAP. I have seen some sticky situations typically because of disagreements or estrangements among heirs or between generations (parents and adult children), and the adage referring to one's health is just as valid for potential family estate disputes, "An ounce of prevention is worth a pound of cure."

The most common situation I have seen that may be problem provoking is between a second or subsequent wife and the adult children, typically from the husband's first wife. The kids sometimes are worried that what they conveniently define as their supposedly rightful inheritance from Dad will instead end up in the hands of Dad's current spouse.

I have seen some adult children genuinely delighted Dad remarried. In the better examples, the adult children successfully maintain positive relationships with their mother, father, and father's spouse. What may facilitate this is if their parents, over time, establish an amicable parenting relationship postdivorce. Angry at your ex-spouse? When one parent denigrates the child's other parent, it can be harmful to children of any age—please vent to a counselor, not to children.

However, it is not uncommon for the children to emotionally side with their mother whom they typically far prefer versus Dad's new wife. The adult children may harbor anger at Dad if they believe that a younger spouse replaced Mom. They may not know or may not like Dad's spouse who, in some cases, may be scarcely older than the adult siblings.

The second or subsequent spouse may be wondering, as their husband may die long before they do, will there be enough assets to take care of her, or will too much of her husband's assets (in her opinion) end up in the hands of her none-too-pleasant stepchildren? Both sides may view the other as a stepmonster since both could see each other as a competitor for Dad's assets, which they may think is more rightfully theirs. Thus, subsequent marriages can be fraught not only with emotional overtones that can poison relationships but also with a financial aspect that, mixing metaphors, can add fuel to the fire.

A skilled estate planning attorney can work wonders in advising you or your family while creating documents, enabling the preferred outcomes and limiting the likelihood of unwanted results occurring.

Years ago, a celebrity was married to his fourth wife. His adult children's mother had been his first wife. The star wanted to discourage a will contest between the adult children and his then current wife. His legal team built a provision into his will in case any of his heirs contested his will. If any of his heirs sought the probate court of the county where the celebrity was domiciled to set aside his will to secure more of his estate assets for themselves, that person or persons would immediately no longer be an heir of the deceased. They would not get a dime from his estate. Unsurprisingly, since immense sums of money were involved, none of his heirs contested his will. Those individuals to whom he wanted his assets transferred upon his death received what he intended them to have since he had sound legal advice.

If we look at what effective estate planning is, though texts have many definitions, the example above shows the heart of it. Here's my unsexy version: effective estate planning enables an individual to expeditiously transfer their assets to whom they wish with as few fees or taxes incurred. Voila!

Please keep uppermost in your mind, if it is your or your spouse's, your parents', or your adult children's situation, at the most basic level, what do you want to happen? Whatever that distills down to, keep your focus on that goal. Then work with your family and your advisers as a team to help you map out the steps needed to reach that destination, for yourself or for those you love.

Many years ago, someone who became a dear friend happened to marry just as the Great Depression began. When I made her acquaintance, her husband had already died, and he had had a simple will. The collapse of the economy during the 1930s left this couple so frightened they became incredibly frugal. Subsequently, they lived in fear of a repeat event, so they became prodigious savers.

Their worry was intense and continual. This couple had seen so much hardship during this terrible economic time in US history that when interest rates soared during the 1970s and early 1980s, paying as high as 18 percent on a money market account (while borrowing rates were at 21 percent, they still held $100,000 ($100K) in cash in their lockbox. They earned no interest on $100K for decades.

They feared scary conditions like the 1930s could return. They witnessed the collapse of some banks, taking depositors' money with them. If they had cash safely on hand, they knew that at least they would be able to afford to eat. At any point, they could have taken their currency out of their lockbox and put it on deposit at the bank, which then had added the safeguards of FDIC insurance on $100K. During the grotesque period of high inflation of the 1970s and early 1980s, they would have earned, depending on the year, $12K, $15K, or even $18K per annum, before taxes, as interest rates skyrocketed.

This hardworking, responsible couple could have more than doubled the amount of their $100K had they put it on deposit, after taxes. However, their prior painful experience had so seared them that it was more important to them to forsake atypically high rates of return for the certainty of currency they could access in just a few minutes as a bank branch was in walking distance from their home. This example shows how deep the wounds of financial collapse can cut into individuals.

A lesson I have learned working with clients is that different individuals, couples, or families place significantly different emphasis on factors like the price they are willing to pay for "peace of mind" or for "convenience." Both can be costly and beneficial. Some individuals decide that a given price for either or both is more than they are willing to pay when weighing cost versus benefit by their metric. Simultaneously, other clients are more than happy to pay for mitigation of their worries or to enjoy greater convenience and ease.

As the ancient Roman expression wisely held, which fits so many situations related to differing preferences, "There's no accounting for taste. To each his own." As will be discussed later, what will be more critical for you or for those you love? Is it doing some of the "legwork" associated with settling an estate to suppress costs to the estate and heirs, or is it instructing their attorney's "back of the house [office]" to handle most of the estate administration work?

The couple mentioned above did not believe in taking on debt. If these spouses couldn't pay for something, they didn't buy it. Neither he nor she had ever had a high-paying job. Based on their relatively modest annual income, they became surprisingly wealthy. Sadly, then alone and grieving, his widow began to receive phone calls she found frightening from people demanding money or who were envious and sought to badger her who had read the will. Had her husband had both a will and a revocable living trust, no one could have learned of her husband's assets when he died via the will. With a revocable living trust, she would not have received such unpleasant, scary calls.

What adult children would do well to consider is that a parent in most cases has no obligation to leave anything to them. I have seen individuals disappointed by the behavior of one or more of their family members either dramatically reduce or even "cut out" from their will and revocable living trust the person with whom they were displeased. This removal occur not only with wills and revocable living trusts but also on traditional and Roth IRAs, for example, where we are aware of changes of beneficiaries.

In a second marriage, the IRA owner, with surprising frequency, changed the primary beneficiary, who was due to receive 100 percent of the IRA account's assets, from their spouse to their adult child and back again something like six times.

Please note that attorneys, not wanting to be falsely accused of malpractice, may advise the person whose will intends to "cut out" one or more of their adult children to mention that child by name and leave them a nominal amount. Why? If that adult child is unmentioned, that adult child may later claim the law firm accidentally failed to list their name. They may argue that their exclusion from the will was merely a typographical error and was not the intent of the deceased.

Along with including in the will the adult sibling's name and token bequest, some attorneys encourage the inclusion of an explanation, even if it is vague, of why that adult child was given so much less of the deceased's estate than their siblings. It may be as simple as, "My daughter, Susan I. Poorer, is to receive two hundred dollars [$200] for reasons of which she is well aware." It is much harder for Susan to prevail in a will contest versus her sibs if she is mentioned in the will and given something tiny as contrasted with her name not appearing in the will, with no reference to her whatsoever.

Also, consider the following situation. Loving parents generously provided one of their children with significant financial assistance. This couple had three children. Their other two children were successful enough that they never needed Dad's or Mom's financial help as much as their sibling did. Mom and Dad want to be exactly fair to all three of their children in terms of the division of their estate. How can they do this?

In this vignette, let's suppose they gave $100,000 ($100K) to the adult child. If they wish, they can have their attorney build into their will or trust that their child who received such substantial assistance is to only receive assets from Mom's and Dad's estate after their two siblings each first receive $100K. Then they equally split any remaining estate assets three ways. Problem solved.

The parents liked their attorney's solution. At least two of the siblings will probably agree that this outcome is equal, and maybe even the third adult child acknowledges the fairness of their parents' estate planning choices.

Wills can be simple as a will has only a few requirements. I read the will of a former US Supreme Court chief justice. Its length was one page and could have scarcely been simpler. A local attorney shared a story of his father who became a municipal court judge and who wrote a handwritten will on a legal pad.

The will must indicate that it is indeed your will. It lets you select whom you would like to serve as an executor of your estate (more on this later). There's also a protective "residuary clause" that covers any of the deceased's estate not explicitly given to heirs or legatees. The residuary clause serves as a catchall provision for any discovered assets of the deceased's estate that are not already doled out using the will. In effect, "And everything else in my estate goes to X."

X could be a "natural person," such as a spouse, adult children, nieces, and nephews; or X could be a "nonnatural person," such as a charity, foundation, or endowment. Often, X is already the intended recipient of those assets listed in the will by type, dollar amounts, or percentages.

If the individual (or couple) who wanted a will created for themselves was advised by their attorney also to create a revocable living trust, then typically that person's will contains a "pour-over" provision. The purpose of a pour-over provision in a will is that assets not already titled or retitled to the name of the revocable living trust pour over to the revocable living trust according to the terms of that deceased individual's will.

Visualize this through a metaphor. Suppose some of your assets were in a beautiful glass pitcher in the form of water (talk about your assets being liquid!). You may own some of these assets—also referred to as being titled—in only your single name (meaning you are the sole owner of those assets).

Let's also suppose that while living, the individual had some of their assets renamed or retitled to their revocable living trust. However, in our visualization, they did not yet retitle all their holdings to or in the name of their revocable living trust, then they died. Since their attorney built into their will a pour-over provision, when they died, the executor of their will then acts to move all those assets not titled or already in the name of the revocable living trust over to their revocable living trust.

Those assets in the revocable living trust will be distributed to the beneficiaries of the deceased's revocable living trust according to its provisions, typically by the successor trustee, who often wears two hats, also simultaneously serving as the executor of the deceased's estate.

Most helpful for anyone who makes a will today is the practice of making a will "self-proving." A father moved from his home state (where he was officially domiciled) to the state where his son lived, where he then became domiciled. Unfortunately, Dad did not choose to repaper his will and other documents in his new "home" state. He created his will many years earlier, and he died in his midnineties.

When his son worked with an attorney to probate his father's estate, they discovered that his father had a will that was not self-proving. As a result, this meant that at least one of the persons who witnessed his father sign his will decades earlier had to confirm their signature—that they did indeed watch this man sign that will. Quite routine. It surprised him that after his father's death that his father had outlived all the witnesses.

In this case, since it was not a self-proving will, it was as if Dad died without having a will. The term for an individual who dies without a valid will is said to have died "intestate." If you have an attorney draw up a will for you, though the attorney creates that legal document, you are the "will maker" (not the attorney); or in legalese, you are the "testator." (I only include this information in case your counsel uses jargon or if you are reading some other work and encounter these terms; otherwise, I would hit your mental Delete key).

Besides witnessing when a will is drawn up, there's one additional step taken to make it self-proving. A notary also is present, watching the signing, so the notary's stamp and signature make it unnecessary to find the witnesses at the death of the testator. Notarizing the will prevents this potential problem!

This vignette underscores the need for you to bring your estate planning legal documents and your beneficiary clauses into your attorney for a review every few years, based on the time line that your attorney recommends, to be sure you remain fully buttoned up. State statutes regarding estates change; litigation occurs, resulting in new case law potentially leading to opportunities for your planning and strengthening your documents. Yes, if your situation changes, please visit your estate planning attorney to inform them to see if anything different needs to be done to protect yourself and those you love.

Though wills are about passing assets from the deceased individual to whomever they choose to receive their assets, wills also can serve in a critical function of which many young parents are unaware. Even if a young couple with children has few, if any, assets, a will can be quite protective. Unfortunately, I have seen simultaneous death three times over my career, so it is not as rare as we would prefer or expect. Two of those were auto accidents of older drivers.

Parents can indicate in their wills, should the tragedy occur that both parents had died, whom would they prefer to raise their child(ren)? Making decisions and caring for the child's well-being are referred to serving as guardian of the child. An individual could be selected by the parent not to raise the child but to handle any assets, like life insurance proceeds, which is available for the child's care, and this role is known as conservatorship. In many cases, parents indicate in their wills that the same person, often a family member, serves both functions simultaneously, though they sometimes are held by two different people (which can lead to disagreements, raising the question, How is a deadlock between caregivers mediated?).

Courts tend to look favorably on the selection by parents of the individual(s) named in a will to care for their children as guardian and conservator. It is often respected since it shows that parents thought it important enough to prepare for an unlikely event, and they indicated whom they preferred. While you may be decades beyond raising children yourself, you may serve your family well as a center of knowledge by letting your adult children or grandchildren or other families know how essential a will can be even when a young couple has scant assets.

The most heartrending true "will" story that I have come across is that of a farmer who fell under his equipment. While bleeding to death, he wrote on his tractor, using his blood as ink and his finger as a pen, that he was leaving everything to his mother. The probate court in his county accepted this as his valid will.

Executors, Administrators, and Personal Representatives

In your will or that of your loved one, you or they indicate whom you want to serve as executor for your estate. This selection is crucial as the executor has an authoritative role. This individual has the enormous task of settling your or your loved one's estate. Typically, there is one executor. Prudently, often the will has a series of successor executors indicated as alternates in case the deceased's preferred executor has died, is ill and cannot serve, or does not choose to serve in this arduous capacity.

The executor is the person that the probate court makes accountable for settling the estate correctly. It requires a high degree of responsibility. Mostly, I have seen one executor in charge of all the tasks, though in some situations, I have seen two or three coexecutors all wielding authority. This shared authority may require all coexecutors to sign each document, which can be an administrative irritant if they live far away from one another.

I often find that clients select a trusted family member, particularly one who lives in the same county as they do. The question that can be faced is what mechanism will, in effect, "break the tie" if there are two coexecutors and they do not reach agreement on what to do regarding some decisions. I have seen in one legal document (an irrevocable living trust) where an attorney offered and the family agreed that if there was a deadlock, the attorney, "without a dog in that fight," presumably could dispassionately decide fairly and break the tie. Some individuals would not want a nonfamily member tiebreaker as the attorney may be wholly unaware of family dynamics.

Many individuals select one person to avoid squabbles, so there is one individual with all the needed authority.

In other cases, my clients have shared with me that they wanted multiple coexecutors, usually their adult children, for reasons such as if all their adult children were coexecutors, it would not seem like favoritism. The reason a given individual may choose to indicate in their will more than one executor was so each coexecutor share the workload for transparency among siblings and, ironically, to prevent squabbles, with each family being unique. I joke with my clients and students that virtually every family says to me something like, "We have special situations in our family, Michael." I reassure them that from my experience, that appears universal.

Ask the person you are considering writing into your will as executor if they would be kind enough to serve. To my surprise, I learned after the death of a client that I was listed in a widower's will as the first and only alternate executor, without my client asking me to serve in that capacity. Though honored that I was named to such a position of trust, no matter how much I would have loved to help, it was a structural impossibility. The deceased's first choice did not want the task, and I am not permitted to serve in such a capacity as it's a conflict of interest, which I would have explained had I been asked. So reluctantly, the initially named executor accepted the task with only two individuals named in the deceased's will.

If you ask someone to serve as executor, tell them if it will be an unpaid or paid position. Nearly always, it is an unpaid position if the executor is a significant heir under the will. Executors may receive a percentage (for example, 5 percent) on the dollar amount of the (typically, of the probate) estate. Each state has its statutes related to all estate matters, and they vary. In one situation of which I was made aware, the family was delighted to pay the executor who, though a family member, was one generation below the heirs he was kin to as he had quite a broad set of tasks to settle the deceased's estate.

Let's discuss nomenclature at this juncture. Thus far in this chapter, I have only referred to the term *executor*. I chose that only because I have found that to be the name with which most laypeople are familiar. However, technically, that refers to a male who is indicated in the will to serve in that capacity, while a female is an executrix. Executrix and executor are equal in authority. If there is no valid will, a female appointed by the court is an administratrix of the estate, and a male appointed by the court when there is no valid will found is called an administrator of the estate. You can see how having four names for the same function—being given the authority to settle the estate—can be confusing.

More sensibly, today, the preference is not to make the distinctions in nomenclature referencing if a person died with a will or without a will or denoting female or male. Today, the preferred term is personal representative (PR), which covers all four prior terms. However, among laypersons whether female or male and whether there was a will or there was no will found, virtually everyone who mentions their role to me still, from tradition, refers to themselves as, "Michael, I am the executor of my mom's estate."

Often when there is no will or a will cannot be found (please note copies do not count), the personal representative, formerly the administratrix or administrator, is appointed by the court as the deceased left no will to direct the probate court whom the deceased wanted to serve as their personal representative. This individual is often a family member, but it doesn't have to be as the probate judge could select someone else to serve in that role. Here's just one reason why having a valid will is so critical: you or your loved one select whom you or they most trust to settle the deceased's estate.

When probate court determined the deceased died with a valid will, the personal representative doesn't have to get the insurance that may be required when there is no will. The purpose of the insurance is to protect the estate, with the presumption being if there is a will naming a personal representative, that person is a trusted, responsible person. The cost of the insurance policy (it's premium payment) is then an expense for the estate to bear.

As an example, one client shared with me that he was going to put into his will his youngest of five adult children to serve as his personal representative, "And I don't care which of my kids doesn't like it, Michael, because by far my youngest will do the best job."

Just one aside that may be helpful: if you are the PR and the contact of various vendors, such as the power provider (electric and gas companies, for example), and you need to explain your loved one died, as soon as you can set up an estate checking account to pay their invoices, you typically will find them understanding. However, you need to notify them, which is a chore.

Sometimes, I see individuals serving as PR becoming anxious over the accumulating invoices for their deceased family member. However, for immaculate accounting, unless necessary, I do not think it wise to use your funds for estate payments. You may choose to ask the financial institution of the deceased what is needed for you, as PR, to open an estate account for bill paying. That's often the most prudent route to take. Many times, the institution can do this reasonably quickly. Ask your attorney if you have a concern.

How do you prove to any institution that you have been given the authority to conduct business for the deceased's estate as PR? If there was a will, then you will receive a one-page document called letters of testamentary (LT), which in effect indicates you are the boss (there's an official governmental seal on the paper). You make the decisions for the estate, and the clerk of court provides that document.

If there was no will, a document referred to as letters of administration (LA) conveys a similar power. So suppose your dad recently died and you want to move some of his checking and money market funds to a new estate checking account to meet invoices, like the water bill, what do you typically need to make this happen? Let's say you visit the bank your dad has his checking account at, usually you will need three items to make this happen. First is a certified copy of the death certificate, which I will discuss in detail later. Then you will also need either the letters of testamentary (there was a valid will) or letters of administration (there was no will). Either document, LT or LA, confirms to the institution that you have the court's authority as decision-maker for the estate of the deceased. You drive the bus. Also, to be sure that it is you, they often will request some form of identification (driver's license, passport) to be sure that you are indeed the person on the LT or LA. Many institutions will make a copy of all three documents. Sometimes, they may need to keep a certified copy of the death certificate, but often, they return that as well. Pretty much everywhere your loved one had assets, a certified copy of the death certificate, the LT or LA, and your ID will be needed.

Then in the hypothetical above, you would be signing the checks. However, that institution indicates what it prefers. They may have you sign your name, or they may request you add John Jones, PR or executor. Ask for their guidance. Also, inquire if they can give you a few generic unprinted checks (which may have a check number on them though no name, such as The Estate Account of X; until the printing of estate account checks) so you can expedite bill paying for the estate.

Once a lot of the bills are paid, I see the attorney advise or the PR decide that they can pay out half to two-thirds of the estate assets reasonably early in the process (maybe a few months after the deceased died, depending on the PR's progress). In prudence, typically the personal representative holds a fair amount of liquid assets just in case of surprise invoices.

Also note, if an individual receives an asset but the estate doesn't have enough money to meet the deceased's debts, some or all the assets conveyed to a given party may need to be redirected by the PR to pay off the deceased's liabilities. I don't see this often, but be aware it can happen. The personal representative has much authority to fulfill their many duties.

My students laugh when I tell them this: "You need to have a will because if you don't, the state of [insert your state's name] has one written for you, which is not nearly as favorable as the will you'd write for yourself." True!

Durable Health-care Power of Attorney
(HPOA) a.k.a. Medical POA (MPOA)

While this document is so crucial for all adults to have, it runs only a page or two in length. As contrasted with some other legal documents, the health-care power of attorney (HPOA or sometimes MPOA for medical power of attorney) is easy for the layperson to understand. In different states, this legal document goes under different names, and I am using them interchangeably.

Though brief, the MPOA or HPOA conveys significant authority and can be so helpful to the person seriously ill and their family. The health-care power of attorney (HPOA) document is one type of advance directive designed to address the following problem. When a person is incapacitated, who will make medical decisions when they cannot make sound decisions or cannot respond?

Using a medical POA, the principal authorizes one or more individuals (an agent or attorney-in-fact) to be able to make those medical-related decisions for them. Typically, there may be one agent or multiple agents authorized by the principal, and often there are several successor agents named in the document.

Sometimes, written into the HPOA document is a HIPAA release form. Alternatively, most of the time, I have seen the HIPAA release as an accompanying one-page document that is a little more than one paragraph, though it too is a vital document.

In 1994, HIPAA legislation was passed by Congress and signed into law by the president. The public focus on this legislation related to an individual leaving one employer and then discovering that their new employer's insurer treated their health issues as a preexisting condition that the insurer at the new employer did not want to cover. This stranded individuals and families without health insurance coverage due to a change of employer. HIPAA improved this issue.

However, when you visit any medical-related office or institution, they either check that you already have a HIPAA release form on file, or even if so, they may have you sign another form. What is the purpose of the HIPAA release form? The concern in the 1994 legislation was about the release of confidential medical data, with related medical personnel at risk of being charged with a felony if they disclosed that which is confidential. So if you sign a HIPAA release form, your signature allows that organization to give the data to appropriate needed additional health-care providers for your benefit without putting health-care personnel at legal risk.

Thus, the combo of a health-care POA with a HIPAA release enables the principal's agent to receive any medical records and instruct the medical provider to send those records elsewhere (because presumably the patient, that is, the principal, cannot do so due to their current health condition). Plus, the principal and family know there is someone, typically a family member, who has the needed authority to make medical decisions for the principal. The person who is the agent for the individual who is severely ill, for example, may choose to replace one physician with another.

Take a copy of both your medical POA and HIPAA release form with you while you travel. It may help you by leaving a copy in the one piece of luggage you always use. However, in case, atypically, there is one trip you don't take that bag, be sure to list that you need to bring a copy of your HPOA and HIPAA release on your standard travel checklist under essentials, as a reminder, despite a copy already being in your travel bag. Leaving a copy in your auto can be helpful.

Some states have chosen to offer online a free version of a state-specific document that serves as the equivalent of an HPOA. One version is called the MOST, and it requires no notarization. The person it covers fills it out on both sides of the sheet, signs, and dates it. It is quick, and the individual's portion is easy to complete.

Their physician also signs it (please read the accompanying online information and directions).

If you do not have a health-care POA already, check online to see if your state offers something that has no cost, at least until you visit an attorney to have them provide you their version. Often having your attorney create an HPOA and HIPAA release is inexpensive.

Also, a service that the bar associations of many states offer once or twice per year is free legal clinics where attorneys volunteer to help anyone, and this may include essential legal documents. Check online at your state's bar association, looking at its events calendar; often, the clinics will be held in different locales simultaneously, or clinic locations may rotate throughout the year.

The colloquially phrased question is, Is the HPOA the "pull the plug" document? No. That document is a living will, discussed in the next chapter.

Advance Directives, "Living Wills," and DNRs

I joke that the US comprises 50 states, and yet there seem like there are 163 different names for a living will across the states. Critically, it is not a will at all as it has zero to do with inheritance. Second, it has nothing to do with living; it is about dying. This legal document has clear instructions to health-care professionals that this individual does not want artificial life-prolonging treatments.

A decision of the US Supreme Court affirmed the right of all Americans to death with dignity. Many individuals choose to have an attorney craft what is broadly referred to as an advance directive to secure this right. The term advance directive includes, for example, both the poorly named living will and a DNR, which is an order by a physician not to resuscitate the patient.

I will refer to the so-called living will more specifically as a desire for natural death document. Your attorney can tell you the official name of the living will–type document in your state, or you can find that information online.

I will artificially divide this document into two types that I have seen. More commonly, I have seen the extended detailed version of the desire for natural death document that has spaces before some of the paragraphs where the person may choose to sign their initials. Doing so indicates that the individual for whom this desire for natural death is drawn up does not want to receive this specific aspect of medical and hospital care. Feeding and hydration are the two most common initialed instructions that the individual may direct in advance to be withheld by the institution and its health-care personnel. A lack of hydration may significantly hasten death.

What I will refer to as the other style of desire for natural death is a page or so in length that, in the most explicit language, unambiguously indicates the individual chooses not to be kept alive artificially through various health-care interventions. Thus, the individual, while of sound mind, instructs (directs) in advance via a desire for natural death document what their preference is regarding the end-of-life medical interventions. This second style does not go into the specifics; for example, there is no reference to feeding and hydration. However, it is crystal clear.

Both styles have been proven effective. Often, the form used is the preference of the attorney. I have had some clients indicate they would not utilize such a document due to their religious beliefs. *I hope this work stirs you to consider your views on end-of-life treatments.*

So many clients over the course of my career have let me know that, as they say it, "Michael, I don't want to be kept alive by a machine when I have nil chance of coming back and being me." If I had to choose a single estate-planning topic where I have found overwhelming agreement, individuals desire to be able to be let go and die naturally.

These documents aid the family to accept that this is what Mom or Dad wanted. That helps mitigate feelings of guilt that are so undeserved but are nearly a universal part of letting go of a dying loved one. This document tends to be inexpensive as it tends to be the same document used over and over by attorneys. It is a priceless safeguard to have for the individual and their family if needed. The medical personnel and the institution are seen to be on safe ground to act with such clear instructions.

The DNR or do not resuscitate document often is the size of letterhead, and it has a bright red stop sign, like the stop sign one would see at the end of any street in the US, in the center of the page. The rest of the page may be a light gold, and the individual's physician signs it.

The physician gives the DNR to the patient who has only six months or less life left. Thus, while the DNR is a type of advance directive, it is not requested by the patient of their legal counsel. The individual seeks it from their physician.

The DNR is often kept near the patient at home, in a prominent place, in anticipation of the arrival of EMT personnel, so the DNR can be shown to them as well as quickly grabbed to bring to the hospital for the medical staff. In the hospital, the patient receives a DNR bracelet, alerting the team of the physician's order to "do not resuscitate."

Please think through your views and wishes as to advance directives, and if you favor a desire for natural death, this critical document is easy and quick for an attorney to draw up; it is often inexpensive for you. You likely will feel significant relief that you have protected those you love.

Who Owns the Property Is Crucial!

You may choose to own property in your name only, sometimes referred to as single-name ownership (or also as "fee simple" ownership). You can own property in joint name with one or more individuals. Also, the third form of ownership is known as placing the assets you choose into a revocable living trust, which your attorney can draw up. You may then decide to retitle assets that are in your single or joint name (provided all the joint owners agree) over to your revocable living trust.

Each form of ownership brings its pros and cons. The implications of each kind of ownership need to be understood, with which your attorney can assist you. As your life needs change, the types of property ownership you use to meet your current living needs may change. Let's look at some examples.

As a hypothetical, suppose you marry, and you and your spouse choose to set up checking, money market, and brokerage account, with both of you as co-owners. Furthermore, you want the certainty of a built-in safeguard that if you die while having assets in any or all those co-owned accounts, your ownership portion transfers to your beloved spouse. The joint tenants with rights of survivorship (JTWROS) agreement is a standard tool that married couples choose to use to own assets that they then place in that specific account. This ownership or titling of the property is designed specifically to transfer the property to the surviving owner(s) upon death. (I will keep repeating both the full name of this form of joint-ownership agreement and its abbreviation to better acclimate you when you encounter it with your attorney and financial adviser).

Thus, once they sign the institution's required document, an account is established, with you being given some identifying numbers or letters to delineate that specific joint account owned by you and your spouse. In the past, it was in the form of paperwork, while today, the completion of digital entry of that institution's required account opening information, once approved by someone at the institution, leads to the opening of this new account. At some institutions, a staffer will do the input for you; at other institutions, you will be required to go online, either at an in-store service kiosk or online from your device (computer, laptop, and phone) and enter the necessary personal data yourself.

Each financial institution has that document available, at no cost, to be used by customers or clients who seek to own assets jointly. You and your joint owner, in this example, your spouse, will either sign using ink or using a digital signature the JTWROS agreement. Ask for a copy and put that in the paper or digital file where you retain your information on that account. This JTWROS may assist you and your loved ones.

Think of the JTWROS account as a "home," receptacle, or container to receive the assets, which the couple or joint owners equally own. Typically, the couple then acts to move some of their assets that is to transfer whatever they wish to own jointly into the JTWROS account that the couple established.

What happens if the death of one of the two joint owners occurs? Though both parties own the assets in the account without doubt, when one of those two dies, it is unquestioned that the surviving joint owner then holds all the assets currently. For clarity, I will use the uncomplicated example of just individuals A and B, who happen to be married, having set up at some financial institution, such as a bank, savings and loan, credit union, brokerage firm, or an insurance company, a JTWROS-type account. Whatever type of property is held in the JTWROS account, whether a joint bank checking, a money market account, or a joint brokerage account, when A dies,

B gets or now solely owns all the assets that are in that account. If B happened to die first, then A, the surviving joint owner of the assets in that account, would receive all the assets currently held there.

Often, married couples own their residential property titled in both of their names as joint owners. At the "closing" as they purchase the property, let's suppose their attorney serves them to be sure all is appropriately done. So upon the death of A, B will own their home, or vice versa.

In this example, did the will have anything to do with transferring the deceased's ownership portion to the surviving owner? No. The will had nothing to do with this situation; it was not the mechanism that led to the transfer of asset ownership from the deceased to the surviving joint owner. The governing document establishing the checking account, money market account, or investment account is a JTWROS agreement.

Please note that not only a married couple may establish a JTWROS type of account, say at a bank or an investment firm. More than two individuals may create such an account for assets to be owned jointly, with survivorship ownership already prepared. I have seen five joint owners, all of whom were family. Also, nonfamily can set up a JTWROS-type account.

It is crucial to be aware of how your will coordinates with your revocable living trust. However, you could either intentionally or unknowingly have your beneficiary designations made out to different primary owners than whom you have indicated will receive assets at your death via the provisions in your will. You may intend this incongruity to occur, or that may not have been your intent. Sometimes, I see a client have all the names of their primary beneficiary in sync with their will (and with their revocable living trust). However, it's not uncommon for clients to earmark some account that has what they consider to be a proper amount of assets with a different primary beneficiary.

Here's an important issue of which to be aware. Suppose your father or mother, or some other relative, neighbor, or friend whom you are assisting decides they can no longer keep up with their financial affairs. You might notice their struggles and ask if they'd like your help with routine tasks, such as balancing their checkbook, paying their bills, and moving funds from their money market to their checking account. How do you go about assisting them?

I have seen it done two ways, both of which work. However, unless you are careful, there's a snare along one of the routes. You can bring a durable financial power of attorney (FPOA) to a savings and loan, credit union, bank, insurance company, or brokerage firm (or to all the above). Typically, if the durable financial power of attorney (FPOA) was drawn up and signed within the past three years, the institution accepts the document after someone in their back office makes sure it has all the formalities of an FPOA. If the durable financial power of attorney (FPOA) was signed by Mom or Dad, in this example, more than three years ago, then the institution may require an additional in-house form signed called a certification of power of attorney.

This certification of power of attorney document also needs to be signed, however, usually by the person who has been authorized to serve as the agent, that is, by the individual empowered by durable financial power of attorney document by the principal. In this hypothetical example, let us presume Mom gave, through her durable financial power of attorney (FPOA) document, the power to her daughter so her daughter could write checks for her. Mom, as the principal who is using the durable financial power of attorney (FPOA) document, gives the authority to her daughter, who acts as Mom's agent in all the ways outlined in the FPOA document.

So the daughter would sign the certification of power of attorney. The daughter's signature as the agent, in effect, assures the financial institution that despite the age of the durable financial power of attorney (FPOA), that is the most current version of mom's FPOA. It's still valid, and the daughter is acknowledging she is the duly appointed agent for mom. The certification of power of attorney protects the financial institution as it has a signed document supporting the durable financial power of attorney (FPOA), indicating the daughter can conduct all business as shown in the FPOA.

The financial institution may also have the daughter sign what is known as a signature card. The daughter's signature uploads to the financial institution's software so when digitally examining the new signature that will appear on Mom's check, the software will recognize it as a valid signature on her mother's check. Instead of by mom, it is by her daughter (as mom's agent) officially as POA. Thus, if the daughter writes Mom's checks, she would sign her name (not Mom's, best to avoid forgery); and then after her signature, she would put a comma followed by an uppercase POA.

As an aside, once, I received a back-office phone call to verify if one of my clients had signed her money market check for a modest sum of money. When you sign a check for household bill payment, during check clearing, a software is digitally examining your signature. If your current signature looks different than the signature card you signed when you opened your account, the software creates an "exception report," which is sent to a staffer for them to examine.

A sweet lady was in her midnineties and was increasingly frail. She had opened her account more than two decades earlier, so her signature no longer looked sufficiently similar as determined by both an automated and escalated human review. When I called her, she confirmed it was indeed her signature. I was impressed because it showed how the system worked to protect my client as well as the custodial firm.

As clients age and become infirm, we see the FPOA route taken often. It is practical and convenient for an aging or ill individual, such as a parent. In the FPOA, one party (the principal) is authorizing the other party (the agent) to act on their behalf as if they were the principal themselves. Typically, the attorney-in-fact or agent is a spouse, an adult child, a brother, a parent, a lifelong friend, or someone else appropriate.

It is vital for the principal who authorizes someone to serve as their "attorney-in-fact" or their agent to be aware that they are conveying immense authority to their agent. The agent is supposed only to do what's permitted by the durable financial power of attorney (FPOA) document, which often is drawn up with broad authority so that the agent can handle any financial situation for the principal's benefit. Only pick someone trustworthy!

The second route also works; however, many times, the individuals, say Mom and her daughter, didn't realize the impact of their choice, possibly creating unintended problems. Months later, a client may convey to me, "Michael, I put my daughter's name on my account at the bank." I know that the client may be referring to bringing the bank a durable financial power of attorney (FPOA). Often, however, that is not what they mean.

Typically, the client put one of their adult children on the account, not realizing that they turned a single checking account into a joint ownership with rights of survivorship type of account. In some situations, this may serve the client beautifully, but in other cases, not so much.

Let's review two hypothetical examples. In the first instance, the husband has died. His widowed wife finds that she is making more mistakes in her checkbook, so she asks her only child, her daughter, to help her write and sign her checks while keeping track of her bill paying. Mom's will leaves 100 percent of her assets to her adult daughter. Mom goes to the bank and asks the banker to put her daughter's name on the account. The banker explains that Mom can put her sole adult child's name on her checking and money market accounts and professionally preps the necessary forms to be signed. Sometimes, individuals do not read standard institutional forms, or even if they read the title of a given form, they may not understand its import. Being accurately told that they could accomplish adding a second name on their account by signing these forms is all that matters to them, which is as human as a human could be.

However, this creates a change of ownership that I have found many clients didn't realize occurred, despite signing joint-account paperwork. It is not that they weren't paying attention; instead, this paperwork is unfamiliar. Did they want a family member to help with crucial administrative tasks? Yes. In many cases, did they intend to change their ownership? No. Moreover, they didn't realize the import or an ownership change, even if aware.

Furthermore, many families do not understand the ramifications triggered by an ownership change. In this example, fortunately, Mom's choice to turn her single-name checking and money market accounts to JTWROS checking and money market accounts without presenting an FPOA to the bank worked perfectly.

Let's look at a second hypothetical. We begin with the same initial facts. The husband has died, his widowed wife asks her daughter, who lives only five miles away, to help her write and sign her checks. Mom has three adult children. However, two of her adult children live out of state.

Mom typically has only $5K or less in her checking account because her bills are modest and there's little yield paid to her on her funds in her checking account. In an abundance of caution, however, Mom has $72K in her money market account. Why?

Mom has been considering moving to a retirement home, and she and her daughter have been scouting out different homes in the area. Knowing a large down payment could be required at some of the retirement homes they have visited but not yet sure which retirement home she may move to, when a jumbo certificate of deposit (CD) for $100K matures at the bank, Mom decides not to renew it just yet. She has the CD and its interest added to her money market account.

Suppose the combined total of the two accounts (checking and money market) is approaching $180K currently. At the bank, as in the first vignette, Mom asks about adding her local daughter's name to her account and uses the same means. Thus, Mom changed her single-name ownership on her money market account into a joint ownership with rights of survivorship type of account. Her daughter now begins to help her with her check writing.

Mom's will leaves all her assets to be divided among her three children equally at her death. Mom is undecided which retirement home to move to; in fact, she's getting cold feet over whether to move at all. She delays a decision but doesn't choose to renew her CD because she's unsure what to do. Her children all want her to be safe, so they are all encouraging her to select a retirement home and move. Unfortunately, during her time of indecisiveness, Mom dies.

Neither Mom nor her daughter realizes the implications of Mom's choice to put her daughter's name on her bank accounts. This task appeared so uncomplicated, even easy. Who now owns all the assets in the checking and money market accounts? Her local caregiver daughter. She currently is the sole owner of over slightly more than $180K of what was entirely her mother's money. This outcome is due to her mother converting the ownership from sole or single ownership over to joint ownership with rights of survivorship accounts, followed by her death.

Her daughter happens to have fair to excellent relationships with her two siblings and, as her mother's executor, knows that Mom wanted all the assets split three ways evenly. Officially, that's not what happened. One of her siblings understands what happened, and the other sibling now gets needlessly suspicious that the local daughter conned Mom into leaving her $180K.

The local daughter never understood that she alone would receive everything left in those bank accounts; she merely wanted to be able to sign checks for her mother's convenience. The local daughter assures her two siblings that she will give them each one-third of the $180K (after paying all estate expenses).

She may want to move some of what's now her money over to an estate account to pay invoices. Now the owner of the $180K must think of gifting rules to properly move funds to her siblings as she has indicated to avoid running afoul of the IRS. Her tax adviser helps her get ready to navigate this task smoothly. Then her husband announces he's filing for divorce and he wants half of her assets, including half of the $180K.

Let's ignore that last unlikely twist. What are some valuable takeaways from the second hypothetical example? Ask if what you are embarking upon is a change in ownership. Although doing so may work correctly for your situation, a brief phone call to your attorney can guide you with the advice you need as to the wisdom of changing ownership or not. Your tax and investment professional may have insight, but neither will be offering you legal advice.

In the first vignette, neither the mom nor daughter understood the implications of Mom's ownership change of accounts from a single name to joint name. It happened that this change coincidentally aligned with the will, so all unfolded as intended, and the process was convenient.

Though the problem of the second situation is solvable, especially since the local daughter honorably wanted to be sure that her sibs both received one-third of what's in Mom's two bank accounts, it becomes unnecessarily messy. It can look bad to the other siblings even though it was innocent. When a loved one just died, avoiding complications and family drama is critical.

After Mom died, the family has enough heartache grieving, plus the local daughter has the headache of settling the estate. When money is involved, some family members can become suspicious quickly over even small amounts. An FPOA could have been used at the bank in either example, so Mom could have the local daughter help her with her check writing, and there would have been no problem at all. The local daughter would never have become joint owner of what was exclusively her mother's checking and money market accounts where $180K was on deposit.

In the second case, the use of the FPOA would have been the much smoother route to take. Repeatedly, individuals are just "putting their adult child's name on their checking or money market accounts," using this means of ownership change for convenience without understanding its implications. Be aware and careful. Ask your attorney's advice on the wisdom of an ownership change versus using the FPOA to achieve the routine request parents or someone infirm makes for help with their checking administration.

The single most significant misunderstanding I have seen the public struggle with is as follows. The adult child's parent dies, and then the family member wants to turn in the FPOA to me for their parent as their financial adviser, kindly thinking it may be useful for me to have. Once the individual dies, their FPOA, in effect, dies with them. It loses all force and effect. Consider it null.

Think of the FPOA being crucial while the individual is alive. However, once the individual dies, then the will spells out who is the executor (also known as a personal representative) for the deceased's estate, and they have considerable authority as well as a significant responsibility. Often, I find that whomever the principal trusted to serve as an agent via the FPOA tool also helps as the executor of the principal's estate.

There's no requirement that the same individual be selected to serve as the durable financial power of attorney's (FPOA) agent and also to act as the executor of the deceased's estate as indicated in their will. However, it often happens that the person who is deeply trusted tends to be asked to do both roles. The trusted individual who is selected often is a family member, and though this is not a requirement, it is a common occurrence. Additionally, it is common that the person asked to serve as agent (attorney-in-fact) on the FPOA and as the executor of the estate tends to be a significant heir of the deceased's estate. That is not required; however, it happens a lot. Consider how that compares or contrasts with your situation or of a family member you may be assisting.

Limited and Full Trading Authorization

Investment and brokerage firms in the securities industry have two forms that clients use to assist someone else with their assets. If Dad has only a single brokerage account, sometimes referred to as a retail account or an individual account, either of these forms may be used to enable someone else, often a spouse or an adult child, to help Dad.

Typically, adding a limited trading authorization form to a client's account is done without cost to the client (the account owner). If the client chooses to sign the limited trading authorization form, their signature empowers whomever they want listed to be able to act to buy or sell securities in their brokerage account. If the client has ownership of five accounts, they can choose to add a limited or full trading authorization form to any or all the investment accounts, as they prefer.

To complete the form, the individual who agrees to serve as the account owner's agent also is required to sign whichever type of trading authorization form (limited or full) is selected by the principal. Let's use the nomenclature you are already familiar with for ease; the account owner whom we'll call the principal signs the form authorizing their agent, whoever is assisting them. The agent also signs the forms, accepting the power to act according to the terms of either the limited or full trading authorization. If the client wants this done on five accounts, then both the principal and agent sign five forms, identified and differentiated by their account numbers.

Please note, limited trading authorization only enables the agent to buy or sell securities only in that account. Most clients prefer to utilize a full trading authorization document to affix to a given account as that empowers purchasing and sale of assets within the account but also adding or removing funds from the account by the agent. In a crisis, this allows the agent to serve the principal in retrieving money from the account for the client's or their family's care.

Again, these are potent documents, so select someone who is most trustworthy and will act only in your best interest. What is excellent about the limited and full trading authorization documents is when added to any brokerage account, the ownership remains the same, unlike changing a single account to a joint ownership with rights of survivorship account.

These come in handy, especially the full trading authorization form, particularly when a client does not have an FPOA. However, both the principal and new agent must sign the type form the principal selected. These forms then attach to investment accounts chosen by the owner, who is the principal. The authorization and the acceptance only impact the assets of the account to which this authorization attaches, whereas an FPOA covers all financial matters, and it is valid wherever the principal has assets. By placing a full trading authorization form on an account, if needed, the agent could liquidate the entire account for the principal.

These forms do not mean that the principal can no longer give instructions in their account. The power of the principal to buy and sell in the limited, and to also withdraw funds in the full trading authorization accounts remains undiminished; there's simply another person who can give instructions. Best of all, either of these two forms is eligible for use on brokerage or investment house accounts in addition to single and joint ownership–type accounts, including traditional, Roth, SEP, and simple IRA accounts. If someone becomes incapacitated and doesn't have a durable financial power of attorney, having named an agent over all the assets in a given client account can be protective of the principal or the principal's family in a crisis.

Beneficiary Designations and Much More

You may find this chapter mind-blowing because you never considered the accuracy of what's below as related to your situation and of those you love. As I teach, I find that most students believe that the document that will serve to direct most of their assets to whom they love at their death is their will. That thought seems most sensible.

For many individuals, this is not so, and people are shocked by this. In some cases, the will ends up conveying few of the assets to the deceased's heirs, depending on how assets are titled, named, or owned. However, as you read this chapter, if this happens to reflect your situation, please do not misinterpret my words as indicating that the will has diminished value or benefit. Not true. The will remains an essential estate planning legal document.

Additionally, beneficiary clauses and designations can be excellent tools for estate planning. Why? A beneficiary designation filled out to a natural person (an individual) to someone you love, like a spouse, adult child, siblings, other relatives or friends, bypasses the probate process entirely. Brava! Bravo! Avoiding probate means your assets in that account or vehicle go directly to whom you indicated as your primary beneficiary.

Alternatively, if the account's (or plan's) primary beneficiary(ies) have predeceased the owner, without the addition of new primary beneficiaries via a change of beneficiary designation form, then the assets go to the contingent beneficiary(ies) if you chose to list contingent beneficiary(ies). If you designate your primary beneficiary to be a nonnatural person, such as a charitable organization, the same excellent outcome occurs. Typically, all that is required for that charitable entity to receive the funds is for the financial institution to obtain a certified copy of the death certificate along with that institution's distribution or termination form, and presto, the charity receives its donation. (The person's estate may receive a tax deduction for the contribution if the receiving entity still meets the IRS's tests as a charitable institution.)

Let's consider where some of the types of entities at which you may have completed your preferred beneficiary designations. You are likely to have beneficiary designations if you have one or more of the following: (a) life insurance policies of any type (term, whole life, or universal), (b) a company-sponsored retirement plan (often referred to as a qualified plan, 401(k), 403(b), 457(b), to name a few), (c) a personal (private, not corporate) retirement account (such as traditional and Roth IRAs), (d) annuities, and (e) a defined benefit pension plan(s). These have beneficiary designations for you to complete to protect those whom you love.

I highly recommend that you consider adding contingent beneficiaries. If you find this encouraging, my accounts have contingent beneficiaries. Check with your attorney on the best way for you to complete each beneficiary designation, both primary and contingent.

When I was a rookie, the only identifying information financial firms required was the name, relationship (spouse, sibling, son, niece, friend), and a mailing address so that the firm could track down the beneficiary. Some firms continue to request only this information.

Today, beneficiary forms frequently require the social security number of all primary and all contingent beneficiaries. A person's address may change twenty times, but since their social security number will not change, it is easier for the firm to find the beneficiary to pay them the proceeds of the account when its owner dies. Also, today, many firms will not let someone establish an IRA account without completing the beneficiary form, though, if they choose to fill in only a primary beneficiary, that typically will suffice.

Sometimes, this is a delicate issue. I have experienced this situation. A client wants to make a nephew or niece a contingent beneficiary. Sometimes, the client feels awkward when calling their relative, explaining why they need their social security number. My tongue-in-cheek dialogue is, "Because I want to list you as a contingent beneficiary on an IRA [or another type of vehicle or account that has a beneficiary designation available], though I want my assets in the account to go to someone else, not you. I want to list you as my least preferred choice, just in case everything I want to happen fails."

It may be a tad sweeter to indicate, "I am updating my estate plans, and I am seeking all the information that could be needed, even in the unlikely event my assets did not pass to my primary [intended] beneficiaries."

Suppose you are completing your beneficiary clause or helping a loved one complete theirs, what will you have to write in or complete by digital entry? Name of the primary beneficiary, relationship (spouse, child, nephew, friend), social security number, beneficiary's address, and crucially important, percentage of account that you are leaving that beneficiary. Typically, the percentage is a whole number from 1 percent to 100 percent. Often, the spouse is the primary beneficiary designated to receive 100 percent; then usually, the designated contingent beneficiary(ies) are adult children set to receive equal percentages. As an example, the co-contingent beneficiaries often receive 50 percent each when there are two children and 25 percent each if there are four children. If there are three children, it is common for two of the children to receive 33 percent with the third receiving 34 percent.

You either will be using a pen, or you will use a digitally generated signature on the application for whatever type of account or vehicle uses a beneficiary designation. Besides your signature, you are writing the date you signed the document. The preference, if possible, is to initial next to the name of the primary beneficiary and initial next to the percentage you are giving that beneficiary. Date both sets of initials. If any dispute arises, you initialed and dated two critical places as well as wrote your signature and the date. This initialing and dating help make sure the person you want to receive your assets as the primary beneficiary receives them. Initial and date the name and percentage boxes of the contingent beneficiary designation as well.

The process is similar for the contingent beneficiaries, who are most often adult children. Sometimes, multiple primary and contingent beneficiaries are listed. If the beneficiary designation form you are signing does not have enough boxes for you to complete, then typically, you add the additional names and information on plain paper or by whatever means the firm you are working with instructs you. If you add a sheet of paper to add other names for primary beneficiaries, contingent beneficiaries, or both, initial and date next to the all beneficiaries' names and the percentage of assets you want them to have, and sign and date the addendum. To prevent this, add on the sheet being separated from the firm's beneficiary designation form. If permitted, on the firm's designation form, write, for example, "See one-page contingent beneficiary addendum with X number of primary or Z number of contingent beneficiaries." We often only see the need for an extra plain paper addendum sheet for additional contingent beneficiaries.

Ask for a copy of both the firm's beneficiary designation form and the addendum page immediately. Please make a copy for your paper or digital file of all beneficiary forms (and any beneficiary attachments) you have signed. Many companies now make this information available online after you enter your private information number (PIN) or pin code into their website.

Gathering and reviewing a copy of all your beneficiary forms allow you to make sure that all those whom you designated as your primary and contingent beneficiaries are currently correct. Also, if you keep a copy of all your beneficiary forms in one file for your executor, you make their work much more manageable. I cannot underscore how often, when I am doing a global asset review with new clients, during the discussion, though they have handed me many statements of their holdings to examine, something unlisted pops into their mind as a result of the thoroughness of our review. Sometimes, it is an asset of surprisingly considerable size, and my observation is not a criticism; instead, it can happen more easily than one may think.

You can save the executor so much time and effort and be sure that no asset goes unexamined if you keep a copy of every beneficiary form in a central file. Should you need to change either a primary or contingent beneficiary form, ask the firm, and a staffer will send you a change of beneficiary form.

It is common that as individuals are gathering and reviewing their beneficiary forms, they realize they need to update their beneficiary designations to reflect their current preferences. Please send a copy to your attorney to be sure that what you have done is consonant with their instructions to achieve what you intend. If you do not take that step, there could be a misalignment between your will and revocable living trust (if your attorney recommends one) and your beneficiary designation.

Think of the investment firm's beneficiary clause as being "a will by contract." Whatever assets are in each vehicle or account are going directly to whomever you have indicated as your primary beneficiary if they are still alive when you die. Was your will involved in the passing of assets using your various beneficiary designations? No, your will has no impact on your beneficiary designations (unless you put as your beneficiary "the estate of _____"). Even if unwisely a person has no will, but they do have most of their assets in accounts or vehicles with beneficiary clauses, then at least those assets will avoid the expense, delay, and publicity of probate and go quickly to whom you love as you intended.

Let's return to the theme that started this chapter. Here's a hypothetical situation with a married couple who plan to retire in one year; the husband is sixty-four years old, and the wife is age sixty-three. Suppose they both had successful careers; here is a snapshot of their current asset totals. They have $2 million total in various forms of term ($1.4 million; some of this coverage they will soon drop) as well as whole or universal life insurance of $600K. They each have a traditional IRA that, between them, totals $400K, and two Roth

IRAs that total $100K. Their two 401(k)'s total is $1.3 million. Each has a defined benefit pension plan, though their companies capped the contributions to those plans during the 1990s. When they gather and review their beneficiary forms, they are pleased to see that on all their separate accounts, they are each other's primary beneficiary for 100 percent, as is so common.

They have not been advised by their attorney to get a revocable living trust, and their will was updated two years ago. They have a brokerage account for $500K that is in a joint ownership with rights of survivorship. Their two accounts held at their savings and loan total between joint-ownership checking and joint money market is $60K. Their home is in joint name as is a small mountain cabin they enjoy (place whatever market value on their home as would reflect the current market value of your property, and likewise for their cabin). They own an SUV, which is in the wife's sole name, and he owns an old pickup truck of nominal value. His employer pays for his leased late-model sedan.

Though seeming to be hale and hearty, the husband unexpectedly receives a diagnosis of stage 4 liver cancer, and he dies six months later. Of all the assets listed above, what assets are subject to the potential delay, expense, and publicity of the probate process? Please scan the list of their assets again and consider this for a moment.

How about the real estate? Their jointly owned real estate is then entirely owned by the survivor. The widow ends up with the single title to their house and cabin—ditto for the checking and money market accounts that are jointly owned so no probate headaches. His life insurance is not subject to income tax and is payable to his wife. Since she's the 100 percent beneficiary, this also avoids probate.

The wife chose to transfer (sometimes informally referred to as a rollover) his (a) 401(k) into her traditional IRA and his (b) traditional IRA into her IRA, which is a right only available to a surviving spouse and also chose to move and consolidate his (c) Roth IRA into her Roth IRA, so none of the IRA funds go through probate. Notice the "like-to-like" transfers (b) and (c) from his traditional IRA to her traditional IRA as a spousal survivor and his Roth IRA transferred to her Roth IRA. I will discuss a critical issue below at length so you can avoid a massive and ruinous mistake.

As she is the primary beneficiary on her husband's pension that he would have later received monthly checks from had he lived, all that income will go to her. Though some pension plans, to relieve themselves of costly future pension liabilities, sometimes offer lump-sum payouts of all pension assets of that individual, which often are eligible to be transferred (a rollover) to a traditional IRA.

A given pension plan may not offer a "take all your money and run" lump-sum distribution option. Alternatively, the pension plan may provide the lump-sum choice, but the widow may choose to receive a monthly check from the pension plan. There's no need for these funds to be subject to the probate process. If she requests a pension check monthly, the widow will pay income tax at ordinary income rates. If the pension plan offers her a lump-sum option that is attractive, she has those funds transferred to her traditional IRA without probate involved.

Their investment account moves to her name only from joint ownership, so no probate process is involved there. What asset is part of the probate process? Only his old pickup truck. That's it, as it is in his sole name. Saying it differently, what of his assets were directed by his will? Only his pickup truck. That's all. Why almost nothing? The beneficiary clauses and designations, those contract-like provisions on the beneficiary forms, were the mechanism that conveyed his assets in those accounts to his widow (traditional and Roth IRAs, as well as his 401(k) and life insurance policies [both term and whole life] and his pension). The joint ownership with rights of survivorship mechanism conveyed the checking and money market accounts, their primary residence, and their mountain cabin to his wife. The only thing the will was for was his beloved truck of modest value.

So his widow makes an appointment with a knowledgeable staffer at their county's clerk of court, which often has wonderfully helpful staff. The clerk of court serves many older individuals. Older voters are the most likely segment of the US population to vote, and the clerk of court is an elected position. After examining all his assets, they look up the make and model year of the truck and receive the dollar value of the truck as the only listed asset of her deceased husband's probate estate.

His will is on file for anyone to examine it, including family, friends, neighbors, coworkers, salespeople, and curious strangers. However, his will indicated that he wanted 100 percent of his assets to go to his wife, which is routine and tells the reader nothing about the deceased's assets. A search of the tax value of the probate estate shows a dollar amount less than $10K. No one knows much of anything (even without the privacy of a revocable living trust), no sales opportunities, no sense of net worth, nothing to make the widow stand out, and virtually nothing to be probated.

I want to alert you to a potentially catastrophic error that you could make that is entirely avoidable. I am asked in class often, "Michael, could I take my 401(k) when I retire and transfer it to a Roth IRA instead of to my traditional IRA?"

If you choose to take your 401(k) or other qualified plan assets (403(b) and 401(a) as two examples) and you transfer those assets to your Roth IRA, 100 percent of the pretax portion of your 401(k) (or other qualified plan assets) will be fully taxable at ordinary income tax rates in the year you elected or received a distribution. This mistake is financial suicide. Let's use hypothetical dollar amounts to illustrate the enormity of this mistake.

You retire. Your company-sponsored retirement plan, a 401(k), has a current market value of $772K. As is often the case today, either all or virtually all your $722K in your 401(k) has never had a cent of it taxed by either the federal government or your state taxing authorities if your situation is similar to the vast majority of qualified plan participants in the USA. Though I will explain how there could be 100 percent of a company-sponsored retirement plan that has yet to be taxed below, please, this is crucial to remember, only if a plan participant has a Roth 401(k) can they transfer and keep tax-exempt their Roth 401(k) assets to their own Roth IRA.

When you find the timing is right, you may choose to transfer all these assets from your 401(k) or other company-sponsored retirement plans, such as a 403(b) to a traditional IRA. Any pretax money that you don't move or roll over (typically in sixty days) are subject to federal and potentially state taxes on the entire pretax amount that you choose not to transfer or roll over to a traditional IRA! It is 401(k) to a traditional IRA. It is not 401(k) to Roth IRA! Red alert. Disaster! It is only Roth 401(k) to Roth IRA; no pretax assets go to a Roth IRA without the pain and burden of full taxation on the entire pretax amount in the tax year of that distribution.

Why have you not likely paid any tax on your qualified company-sponsored retirement plan of which you have been a plan participant, maybe for three decades or longer? Let's suppose you choose to make 100 percent pretax contributions every year you were a plan participant. What does this term *pretax* mean? Let's say that each pay period you contribute $100. It appears that the whole $100 are added to your 401(k), for example, as it is not then taxed by federal or by state taxing authorities. Though please note, while you do not pay fed and state income tax of your 401(k) contributions that you choose to code as pretax, you still pay FICA and Medicare tax on the $100, so not the entire $100 enters your plan as a contribution.

This levy is not as bad as it may sound, at first, since paying the 6.2 percent FICA to the Social Security Administration on your retirement plan contribution in addition to the remainder of your salary or wages means that your eventual social security monthly checks will be more sizable as a result. You are painfully aware, if self-employed, that you are paying in 2019 6.2 percent and 1.45 percent (7.65 percent total) twice—once as the employee and once as the employer. Ouch!

Why do most plan participants choose to make 100 percent pretax contributions to their employer-provided retirement plan? They do it for two reasons: to help them have a lower income tax bill now in each year that they make pretax contributions and to provide their employer-sponsored retirement plan with more "seed corn" sooner.

By contributing pretax, the amount of their contribution or the dollars that enter their retirement plan is more considerable.

Let's look at an example where I will purposely be a bit imprecise to make the concept easier to understand. Suppose in 2019 you are in the 24 percent federal tax bracket. If you contribute $100 to your 401(k), then $100 ends up there (except for 6.2 percent FICA and 1.45 percent Medicare payroll taxes). You have more capital invested sooner to enhance your retirement plan value over time if you choose to make pretax contributions.

If you instead chose to make after-tax contributions and your marginal tax rate (your highest current federal tax rate) is 24 percent, then only $76 per hundred would be contributed to your company-sponsored retirement plan. In 2019, you still must pay the 6.2 percent FICA and the 1.45 percent Medicare tax. However, the levy is against the $100, not the $76.

So it's easy to see, the higher your tax bracket is, the more dollars will be siphoned off by the government for taxes in the current tax year coming out of your contribution amount each pay period. (To make the example more explicit, I supposed all an individual's dollars are taxed uniformly at 24 percent, which is not the case since we have what is known as "a progressive tax system." This term means that the more you earn, the higher your tax rate is, up to a current maximum tax bracket of 37 percent at the federal level. The effective tax rate we all pay is a blend or composite of all the tax rates our income passes through, and it is lower than your last or highest tax bracket, which is called your marginal or top tax bracket.)

Let's look at this same issue using a different example. If you make $60K per year but contribute $10K to your 401(k) on a pretax basis, you report your income as if you earned +$50K, not $60K. Yeah! That is tremendously advantageous for most individuals and families. Since you are not currently taxed on that $10K (that is the difference between your $50K and $60K), it is crucial to remember that Uncle Sam and most states are salivating over being able to tax you later when you are a happy retiree and begin taking distributions from your various retirement plans, such as a 403(b) or 401(k).

We cannot discount the advantage that an after-tax contribution could afford you later. So let's return to the example above. If this year you made $60K in salary and you made $10K in after-tax contributions into your employer-sponsored retirement plan, you would report that you earned $60K, not $50K, to Uncle Sam and your state as you did not choose pretax contributions. For the sake of illustration, suppose only $7.6K of the $10K you contributed to your 401(k) plan for that year arrived in your retirement plan due to taxation. That amount has been taxed already so when you distribute those funds, maybe years later, the $7.6K will exit tax-exempt. This tax-exempt distribution occurs not because the government gave you a tax break on those dollars but instead because you already fulfilled your tax obligations for that sum of money.

So despite some of the money in your company-sponsored retirement plan later favorably exiting as tax-exempt, most individuals want the current year advantage of a lower reportable income to reduce their income tax bill, and they want that advantage repeated year after year. Plus, often, the plan participant wants to contribute as much into their plan as they can afford, as soon as possible, to give their capital the potential advantage of long-term investing, though there are risks to investing.

Suppose that you or your loved one are like most of the plan participants in the US and you or they are making 100 percent pretax contributions. The money you have chosen to be debited from your paycheck to contribute to your employer-sponsored plan, thus, has not been taxed yet by Uncle Sam or at the state level. If your employer makes a matching contribution to your retirement plan, your employer's contribution for you, those funds have had no taxes deducted by either the federal government or by state levels. Any growth in the capital has yet to be taxed. For example, let's suppose you have stock market–related investment vehicles within your corporate retirement plan, which have grown in market value. You have not paid any tax on that capital growth yet. Likewise, if you earn any dividends or interest in your 401(k) that has yet to be taxed, thus, you may have a significant pile of money that can produce sizable monthly income when you retire. As an investor, you may prefer to leave the principal amount undistributed to serve as your retirement income generator.

What does the typical plan participant investor do when they retire to live well? They take monthly distributions from their various retirement plans that typically have been tax-deferred for many years, and they start to use the income generated from or off that money and their social security payments to live comfortably. If they have any defined-benefit pension plans, many of which were or are still so helpful to retirees, these can serve as an excellent source of retirement income.

Monthly social security payments, company-sponsored plan distributions, IRA distributions, as well as personal investment and savings accounts all can coalesce to produce steady income. Getting the timing of distributions right and determining when it is best to take social security checks are critical. Talking with a knowledgeable investment and tax adviser can help you do this prudently so you get what you need and want without incurring undue tax burdens.

Suppose all the money added to your 401(k) was pretax dollars. Once distributions commence, all the funds distributed from the 401(k) are subject to federal and state income taxes (where taxable). How do you know what the total of your distributions is during that tax year? It likely shows monthly on your official statement and probably also on your computer. Additionally, as required by the IRS, the retirement plan mails a 1099-R, with the *R* referring to *retirement*, by the end of January for any distributions received during the prior tax year. You or your tax adviser then lists the total dollar amount of your distributions on your federal 1040 tax reporting form. Similarly, your retirement plan itself reports that same information that you receive to the IRS.

If you made a series of after-tax contributions into your 403(b) or 401(k), only the principal amount of your plan contribution would exit tax-exempt. That is because you already paid fed and state taxes on those contributed funds for the tax year in which you made your contribution. However, in a tax-deferred retirement plan, whether corporate or personal, you shield your asset growth, interest income, dividends, as well as your employer's matching funds from current taxation. You have yet to pay taxes on those funds. Those assets are under custody in your retirement plan on a pretax basis, with one exception unless you utilized a Roth 401(k), which exists but never gathered much momentum and has relatively few plan participants.

Why did the Roth 401(k) not become popular despite its advantages? Most plan participants want the lowest current income tax burden they can have each year. Moreover, they also desire the most contribution dollars to enter their plan each year to help their plans grow well over time, hopefully.

Repeatedly, with careful thought, without investing too much time or effort, by using mechanisms like beneficiary clauses, joint ownership with rights of survivorship accounts, as well as payable-on-death (POD) and transfer-on-death (TOD) tools (which we haven't reached yet but we are nearly there), clients have been able to protect their spouse, adult children, or others they love. The assets moved much more quickly than they would have through probate, so the widow had access to much of her husband's portion of their net worth sooner if needed.

Those mechanisms didn't invite publicity; there's no public information on assets transferring via beneficiary clauses and joint-ownership forms. There typically are no fees for the beneficiary forms or joint-account JTWROS forms. It was easy and quick to complete the forms. This route proved uncomplicated and yet can work so effectively and smoothly. Yes, the example is hypothetical. However, I have seen similar versions often.

Now let's contrast this vignette to your situation, what percentage of your estate assets may transfer to whomever you love using beneficiary designations and joint ownership? Contrast that with how much transfers to an heir is due to your will. Then ask yourself, Is there any incongruity that's unintended between your will and those contract-like mechanisms? If so, have your estate planning attorney advise you how to repair the mismatch if that arose unintentionally.

Since the topic is beneficiary designations, let's look at the statistics of who dies first. If you are male, here's a sobering stat: 75 percent of the time, you will die before your female spouse. Women may be smiling because only 25 percent of the time will women die before their male spouse. The reasons for this phenomenon are not entirely understood. Often, males are indeed older than the women they marry, and that is undoubtedly part of the equation but is only one variable. Also, the reality is that some males (up to 30 percent) are disinclined to get regular medical physicals and other types of wellness and preventive screenings, leading to the belated detection of medical problems. When I learned this years ago, I wondered if that is true. What I have found for more than thirty-five years serving many couples is that the stats are accurate. This likelihood is a salient consideration in retirement planning.

Does the male have a terrific check-a-month life-defined benefit pension plan payout? What pension option did he select? For example, he may have chosen a slightly reduced pension check for himself so that his wife could receive a check that may be cut in half when he dies. This monthly pension payout election is a joint and 50 percent pension election option. If he does die first and if he and his wife happen to own a home, does the county they are domiciled in typically send a note of condolence to his widow indicating they will, henceforth, cut her property tax in half? I haven't seen that yet.

Who lives the longest of any group? Single, never-married women, which doesn't say a lot for husbands. The implication is that not having two incomes, and though it is changing that historically, women have earned less than men. This often leaves single, never-married women with more modest assets as they retire. Since they are the most likely of any age-group to be retired the longest, unless they are left an inheritance, single, never-married women may be the most vulnerable to running out of money before they die.

"Payable to the Estate Of . . ."

While almost all beneficiary designations I see are filled in with a natural person as the primary and contingent beneficiaries, such as a spouse, adult children, and other relatives, occasionally someone chooses to list the primary beneficiary as "Payable to the estate of M. Unwise." Your attorney may judge that there are sound reasons for you to make your primary beneficiary "Payable to the estate of . . ." However, I would only make a beneficiary election "To the estate of S. O. Foolish" with the advice of counsel. Why?

The beauty of naming a natural person—usually someone the deceased loved—as the primary beneficiary is that those assets avoid probate. If the deceased made their primary beneficiary a nonnatural person like an endowment or charity, their assets conveyed using a beneficiary clause also avoid probate.

The benefit of a beneficiary clause is that the death benefit payout of a life insurance policy as well as the entire proceeds in IRAs and corporate retirement plans, such as 401(k)s, go directly to someone the deceased wanted to have the money expeditiously.

Since those often-substantial assets conveyed by beneficiary clauses and designations avoid probate, there are no fees, taxes, delays, publicity, or inclusion in the probate estate of the deceased's related assets. That is an essential aim of beneficiary clauses—to keep all those assets out of the deceased's probate estate. Thus, the transfer of assets is direct, quicker, private, usually without the expense with only minor cost, while leaving the probate court and clerk of court out of the picture. In most cases, this is so much better an approach to make the beneficiary(ies) a natural person, such as a spouse, adult child, or other individuals. Please get the advice of your attorney.

As a notable aside, sometimes, those under age eighteen are listed as the primary beneficiary or, more frequently, as contingent beneficiaries. I have seen the years pass and that child reach the age of majority. If they receive the funds left by the deceased using the beneficiary clause as adults (age eighteen or older), the transfer of assets flows smoothly. Where a potential problem crops up if the beneficiary is under age eighteen when the deceased dies, someone else must step into the picture to help the child. A child cannot own more than a trace amount of assets, and typically, an adult relative makes decisions about assets benefiting the child. It can be messy to get everything arranged. I don't see many children listed as beneficiaries, but when it does occur, they are invariably contingent beneficiaries.

There's one other land mine to avoid. If you are considering listing a trust as a beneficiary, please get the advice of a legal counsel before doing so. Suppose an individual writes on their beneficiary form that their primary beneficiary, for example, of their traditional IRA, is to be a trust, then unless advised to do so by their legal counsel, typically at the IRA account owner's death, all the assets in the IRA have to be disbursed to that trust. Designating a trust as the primary beneficiary may result in losing the benefit of tax deferral on those assets. Potentially, this distribution from the retirement account could create a large and unnecessary tax bill in that tax year; please be careful about this. I would not only seek legal advice but also tax and investment advice if this is your plan or the plan of someone you are serving as a caregiver as this could become an incredibly costly mistake.

PODs and TODs
Payable-on-Death and Transfer-on-Death Beneficiary Designations

The payable-on-death (POD) form is a type of beneficiary clause and designation form offered at no cost by institutions where you choose to put your money on deposit, such as at credit unions, savings and loans, and banks. Let me start with a distinction. Suppose in this hypothetical example that you have a single-name or single-ownership checking account, a single-name or single-ownership money market account, and three different CDs or certificates of deposit, all just in your name or in the title or ownership of someone you love at a local bank. Furthermore, we'll suppose the first CD matures in six months, the second in twelve months, and the third in two years.

Often, the checking account has an individual account number. The money market also has a different account number, which only references the money market, and the three CDs all have unique account numbers as well. The official monthly bank statement may list each of their account numbers indicated immediately to the right of the name of the checking and other accounts.

Contrast this with an investment firm. Typically, it will have an account number for a single account. However, there can be one, seven, nineteen, thirty-two, or any number of different types and quantities of investment vehicles all "attached to" or under that same account number—under the single ownership of you or your loved one. At a financial services firm, a brokerage firm, and investment house, typically, they will have available for you to use if you wish a TOD or transfer on death form. It has a similar aim to the POD above; its purpose is to allow the owner of the single account, in this example, to add a beneficiary clause and designation to an account that for many decades did not have the option or capability to add a beneficiary clause and designation.

On all this, just as you will find on the various issues in this work, each state has its statutes, and each institution gets to make its own business and policy decisions within that state's laws. Let's now say that the individual who has single ownership of five different account numbers at the bank wants to designate a beneficiary on her checking account, money market account, and each of her three certificates of deposit. For simplicity, this individual has only one adult child, her daughter. Typically, though each institution has its policies and procedures, it may require the completion of five POD forms. This task sounds daunting, but it is easy and quick for the institution's personnel and comfortable for the client since through word processing, the staffer can probably quickly prepopulate the same data five times on five forms, with the only difference being that on each form, the account number is unique.

The owner of the checking, money market, and each of three CDs would be signing five times and writing the date five times on that firm's payable-on-death (POD) form. If that were you, please ask for a copy of each POD form you signed and dated for your beneficiary form file.

It is likely when the single owner of those five accounts receives her next monthly statement, there will likely be a notation that each of the five account numbers has added a POD form, which in this hypothetical example has only one beneficiary at 100 percent—the single owner's daughter.

There may be a catch that I will make you aware of; however, there may not be an issue. It depends on how a given institution chooses to handle what's next. While the POD would likely remain the same for the checking or money market accounts, presuming the owner of those accounts doesn't choose to designate a new beneficiary if the account is open for twenty more years, there may not be anything the beneficiary needs to do on either the checking or money market accounts. I have met individuals using the same institution for more than half a century as a satisfied customer.

The possible snag that you need to be aware of, which the staff will be able to answer, is when each CD matures, does that institution require that a new POD be signed and dated for each new CD established? Often the answer is yes because each of the three CDs had their unique account numbers until those three CDs matured. As Mom choose to renew her CDs, the institution issued her a new account number for those new CDs.

Returning to the same hypothetical example, if Mom wants a POD on each of the latest CDs, then she completes a new POD form, which she signs and dates if Mom wants her daughter to be a primary 100 percent beneficiary on the new CDs. If that is a situation that could impact you, ask that firm's personnel if they have a more uncomplicated remedy or if you have to be responsible to remember to complete, sign, and date a new POD at each renewal of a certificate of deposit. This problem is eminently fixable; it just requires someone to remember this—usually the customer. Ask the staffer if the firm has a customer alert reminder system that notifies Mom to complete a new POD every time she renews a CD or establishes a new CD.

If we look at an investment firm that is under different regulations and statutes, if Mom owned a single account with eleven investments of various types, having one TOD form, just one transfer-on-death form applies to all eleven investments in the account. Mom may sell two of the eleven investments held in Mom's single-ownership account and acquire five more investments. However, if this occurred in that separate single account in this hypothetical illustration, Mom doesn't need to redo a TOD. Let's say Mom dies thirteen years later and she hasn't closed that account. Mom also hasn't changed her beneficiary designation on the TOD. Thus, her daughter would receive just as it currently is, whatever investments Mom had in her single account. That individual account now passes without going through the expense, delay, and publicity of probate over to her daughter, who soon becomes the individual owner.

How does the daughter claim ownership of the account and its assets? At the brokerage firm, the daughter brings a certified copy of her mother's death certificate, and she presents an acceptable form of identification, most often a driver's license. Then the daughter instructs the investment adviser what to do with her assets.

The daughter can choose to liquidate the account and receive a check for all the proceeds. If the daughter wants to open a new single account, after a discussion about the daughter's risk tolerance, investment goals, and time horizon, once she signs the paperwork, she will have opened the new single-name or single-ownership account. With a TOD in place, the process could scarcely have been more straightforward.

Once what previously were her mother's investments have been transferred to the daughter's ownership, for the example, let's continue with single ownership for the daughter, if she wishes, she can change some of the investments within the account that better fits the daughter as opposed to what was best for her mother. The daughter can take some money out of the account to spend for whatever she wishes as she is the account owner solely, so she is the boss. All the assets in the account are hers to do what she pleases with just as her mother intended, and it couldn't have been easier.

The daughter can choose to transfer the assets to a joint ownership with rights of survivorship account or a revocable living trust if she prefers. Suppose she kept it as a single-ownership account, she may decide to put her only child—her twenty-five-year-old son—as her primary beneficiary and 100 percent owner on a TOD form that she adds to her new single investment account.

The same ease and convenience exist for the five single-ownership accounts (checking, money market, and three CDs) with five POD forms mentioned in the hypothetical above. Again, all the daughter needs to do is give the bank staff a certified copy of the death certificate, show a valid ID, and give instructions on what to do with her assets.

Both the investment firm and bank may be able to return the certified copy of the death certificate to the daughter after they have made a copy of it for their institution. All TOD and POD forms avoided the probate process on the assets in all these accounts in the hypothetical, plus it made it so much easier for the daughter to retrieve what her mother wanted her to have and enjoy.

There is one significant snare that I want to alert you to that may occur depending on the statutes in your state and depending on what the POD and TOD forms indicate. Please send a copy of each institution's POD and TOD beneficiary clauses as well as your intended designations to your attorney so you avoid this snare below.

While sometimes I see a single 100 percent primary beneficiary as in the hypothetical above, it is far more common for me to see situations where one of the spouses has died and the surviving spouse now elects to put their adult children on as primary beneficiaries. PODs and TODs may seem straightforward like a life insurance, IRA, 401(k), annuity beneficiary clause, and designation, but it may not be at all, so please be careful.

Let's use a different hypothetical to underscore what could be such a significant problem that some individuals are wisely advised by their attorneys not to use either or both a POD and TOD, depending on their circumstance. Suppose Mother has died and Dad is still living. He and his wife have three children, now all adults, two sons and one daughter. Dad doesn't check with an attorney knowledgeable on estate matters. Dad's friend told him about PODs, but Dad's friend has only one adult child.

Dad lists all three of his adult children as primary beneficiaries with the percentage split 33 percent, 33 percent, and 34 percent, which happens to be the closest that institution can divide the beneficiary-designated portions (a whole percent is standard). Suppose that each of his three adult children has families of their own and Dad is a proud grandpa of ten grandchildren.

Tragically and unexpectedly, one of the three adult children dies. Beset with grief; the last thing Dad was thinking about was updating POD beneficiary forms. Dad had told the surviving spouse of his deceased child that she would be well taken care of from his assets when he died as she would receive one 33 percent. Then Dad died.

As it turned out, since one of the three beneficiaries on the POD was now deceased, the two remaining beneficiaries each received 50 percent of Dad's various POD accounts and the wife of Dad's deceased son received none of that money Dad had set aside for all three families by means of the POD beneficiary forms. Therefore, it is so crucial to send all beneficiary clauses and designations you have already completed to a skilled legal counsel. Your attorney can advise under what circumstances it is *not* advisable to use the convenient POD and TOD forms.

Crucial Beneficiary Issues

When an individual dies, their beneficiary(ies), which they listed on the various beneficiary designation forms, receive the deceased's assets. The deceased may own personal and employer retirement plans, life insurance policies, and assets at firms such as banks and securities firms. To get our arms entirely around beneficiary designation forms, we need to make a series of distinctions.

Many times, the primary beneficiary is a spouse, and if the couple has children, they often list their adult children as contingent beneficiaries. Alternatively, the beneficiary may be someone unrelated to the account or asset owner who died. There are unique advantages available only when the beneficiary who receives the assets of the deceased is their surviving *spouse*. Some of those salient advantages do not apply to nonspousal beneficiaries, such as adult children. For example, this distinction impacts spousal and nonspousal beneficiaries who receive IRA assets (such as traditional and Roth IRA assets) differently.

The next distinction is that some retirement plans are for employees of for-profit corporations. There are other retirement plans specifically designed for employees of nonprofit organizations. Where do we get such memorably sexy titles (not!) for employer retirement plans, such as 403(b), 401(a), 401(k), and 457(b) plans?

If you were to go to the IRS website to examine the part of the tax code–numbered section of the 401(k), this section would list all the IRS rules about this specific type of employer-sponsored retirement plan. Typically, the 401(k) retirement plan is established by a company for the benefit of the employees of that for-profit corporation. The company is known as the retirement plan sponsor. Often, the company invites an outside company to provide both the 401(k) plan itself and the investment choices available in the 401(k) for employee selection.

There are employer plans that follow the rules of code section 401(k) that are sponsored by entities that are not "for-profit" companies. As an example of one sizable exception, the state of North Carolina is a plan sponsor of a 401(k), which we typically associate with for-profit companies.

Not-for-profit employer-sponsored retirement plans are often, though not always, 403(b)-type plans. A 403(b) retirement plan follows the rules that the IRS has outlined in that section of its code. Initially, teachers were the primary plan participants in 403(b) plans. Over time, other nonprofit organizations established retirement plans for their employees, also under code section 403(b). At some not-for-profit hospitals, the nursing staff may be eligible to participate in the hospital's 403(b) plan as an example.

Municipal workers use 457(b) plans. These 457(b) plans offer municipal employees unique features that other retirement plans do not offer since no one ever chooses to become a municipal employee to become wealthy.

The next notable distinction is that the deceased may have established and contributed their dollars to their retirement plans. Common examples of popular private or personal retirement plans are traditional and Roth IRAs. Officially, the acronym IRA stands for individual retirement arrangement, but informally, mostly IRAs are referred to as individual retirement accounts. The individual's employer is not involved in that individual's IRAs.

In employer-sponsored retirement plans, such as 401(k)- and 403(b)-type plans, the eligible employee hopefully (wisely) chooses to be a plan participant. The employee decides how much of their wages or salary to contribute each pay period to the specific plan available. Unfortunately, not all employers offer their workers an employer-sponsored retirement plan.

The dollar amount the employee selects is digitally removed from their check each pay period and is added (contributed) to their employer-sponsored retirement account. EFT, electronic funds transfer, debits employee paychecks to make company retirement plan contributions.

Adding your money into either a personal or employer-sponsored retirement plan is "making a contribution" or contributing to your retirement plan. When you remove or withdraw funds from an individual or employer-sponsored retirement plan, that is known as "taking a distribution" or distributing money or assets from your retirement plan(s).

Simultaneously, you may have established and been making regular contributions into your retirement plans, such as traditional and Roth IRAs. I hope that you are making sizable contributions into your employer-sponsored retirement plan each pay period so that between your employer-sponsored and your retirement plans, you enjoy a comfortable retirement.

Both personal retirement plans and those plans sponsored by the employer are tax-deferred. Tax deferral is a fabulous attribute of retirement plans as we will see in a chapter up ahead. It is imperative if you are a caregiver that your loved one, who is the account or plan owner, be certain that their primary and contingent beneficiaries are up-to-date. If your loved one (or you) on your retirement plans want to change the beneficiary currently designated on the beneficiary designation form, the responsibility to do so falls on the account owner. However, that same responsibility to update who the owner now wants as their primary and contingent beneficiaries is also true of life insurance, pension, and annuity beneficiary designation forms, to name three critical examples.

In short, whether it is you or someone you love, please review all beneficiary designations to ensure that they are indeed current. Also, it is frequently quite useful to include on a beneficiary form not only a primary beneficiary(ies) but also a contingent beneficiary(ies).

Each plan or company has a change of beneficiary form, which is increasingly a digital form, that is quick and easy to complete. I have seen beneficiary form changes or updates made by retirement account owners because their primary or contingent beneficiary predeceased them, or sometimes they divorced them, or the account owner experienced displeasure with a recipient. (Be kind to your loved ones! You may be surprised how many times I have seen a client upset with a family member alter their will, revocable living trust, or beneficiary designation.)

If you are the caregiver helping someone using a durable financial power of attorney, if the language of the FPOA is clear and robust, you may be able to change the beneficiary named on a beneficiary designation form of the principal (the account owner). However, in some states, only the individual account owner may change the beneficiaries on their retirement plan accounts. In some situations, if the FPOA were attempting to change the selected beneficiary to themselves, this may not fly.

Caution: if a beneficiary change appears needed and the issue relates to the question, Is the account or plan owner of sound mind? possibly impeding a change in beneficiary, please seek the advice of a skilled attorney. It is so crucial for a person in failing health, particularly cognitively, that all their beneficiary designations, primary and contingent, are current.

Next, our focus is to understand what unfolds after the death of the policyholder or retirement account owner. What do you need to do next if you are the beneficiary and the asset owner of the account or plan or asset has just died? What do you need to do?

Two initial steps need to be taken by the beneficiary, possibly with the assistance of the executor, who often is among the most significant beneficiaries, and heirs. First, death certificates need to be obtained by the beneficiary or the executor. Second, the beneficiary or executor (or their financial adviser on their behalf) requests the institution to send plan or company forms to them.

These forms come from the retirement plan or from the companies (insurance companies for life insurance policies) where the deceased had assets. The beneficiary(ies) is to complete these forms and return them to the institutions. These forms are instructions by the beneficiary indicating what the firm is to do with the beneficiary's new assets or dollars.

The forms I am referring to typically relate to the distribution (payout) or transfer of the deceased's assets to the beneficiary. So for now, think about just two parts of this confusing process—death certificates and the institutions' forms. Please note, these forms can vary considerably in purpose, length, and especially complexity.

Typically, the executor must receive several death certificates to complete their duties successfully. Then if the family is up to the task, each company or retirement plan is notified, usually by phone, that the plan or asset owner has died. Notification of the deceased's death before the issuance of a death certificate is not a requirement. Consider notification as an extra step, though a valuable step to take.

I am empathetic that the bereaved scarcely want yet another unfamiliar chore after their spouse or parent has died. However, if the family itself or their financial adviser undertakes the task of phoning institutions to notify them that the owner of the assets under custody with that firm has died, doing so sometimes yields significant advantages for the beneficiary. If the family makes notification calls, typically, the family caller cannot be given any specific information about the contents of the deceased's accounts. To maintain confidentiality, since the firm is just learning of the deceased account owner's death verbally, the firm likely will not provide any specific information.

For our clients, we prefer to take on those tasks. At a minimum, we verbally notify each institution. Our notification to the firms is not official. Why not? We haven't yet received certified copies of the death certificate from the executor.

Most commonly, the surviving spouse, the beneficiary, the executor of the deceased's estate, or an adult child may notify, for example, a life insurance company that the insured policyowner has died. Unless the retirement plan, asset company, or insurer receives a death certificate, nothing is official from the perspective of an institution. The firms have no proof the deceased has died until they have the death certificate.

While the phone call from family or adviser to the institution is not essential, it is both courteous and may prove quite helpful. It is common that the family is both so emotionally overwhelmed and has so many other more pressing tasks to complete that notification is not done promptly unless a financial or insurance adviser volunteers to help with that chore. If you could use that help, ask them.

The beneficiary may call the insurance company to receive life insurance proceeds, for example. It's best if you have a statement of the deceased's policy or account number before you call as many phone systems want you to either say or enter the policy or the account number. Typically, they ask you for the last four digits of the social security number of the deceased. If you happen to know the deceased's PIN (personal identification number), you probably will be forwarded to an automated information system where you may hear the current value of the assets that you will be receiving as the beneficiary(ies).

If you find yourself having difficulty sorting through the robotic maze of phone choices, referred to as a phone tree, if you dial zero on many systems, that selection often takes you directly to a company representative. Life insurers often have a choice on their phone tree ("Press four") to speak to the death claims department.

Sometimes, family (or their adviser) can glean useful procedural direction from that institution's staff. Employees from an insurers' death claims departments typically have much higher knowledge than a beneficiary may receive from frontline representatives who answer initial phone calls. I have found the death claims staff at many firms to be excellent.

Also, the notification-of-death phone call may expedite the sending of critical forms that I alluded to earlier. Notification can speed up the distribution of assets to the beneficiary(ies) and the transfer of assets to the beneficiary's name or ownership.

Let's dive deeper into step 1: the issue of death certificates. Over my career, I have seen death certificates being issued in as few as three days after the deceased died. On average, I have found that the surviving spouse or the executor or someone appropriate in the family receives the certified death certificates in ten to fourteen days. When something is irregular, I have waited many months to receive a death certificate from a family member of the deceased.

Most people I have served, whether they sought a cemetery burial of the deceased's body or the increasingly popular choice of cremation, used the services of a funeral director. Typically, one of the many tasks of the funeral director is to request the death certificates from the county government on behalf of the family. Then the funeral director may deliver them so the family has what it needs for asset transfer or retrieval (distribution). The funeral director then adds the cost of each death certificate ordered onto the funeral bill.

For example, in our county presently, the cost is ten dollars for each certified copy of the death certificate. I urge my clients to order ten death certificates as I have found that number large enough to meet their various needs. This number may obviate the need for the family to order a second batch. So the funeral director would show in the invoice sent to the family an additional charge of one hundred dollars, in my example, for the death certificates. If a deceased's estate has few assets, you may only need five death certificates, for example.

Sometimes, family members may say to me, "Michael, when can we start the process of transferring Mom's [or Dad's, my spouse's] money into accounts in my name?" That question is on point. However, nothing significant is permitted to be acted upon by any institution until it receives a certified death certificate (or sometimes referred to as a certified copy of the death certificate).

This "holdup" will surprise (and sometimes annoy) beneficiaries or heirs because they know I am aware their loved one died since I attended the wake or gathering of family to mourn the loss of the deceased as well as to respect and to celebrate their life. "Michael, why can't your team submit the paperwork to your home office?" A fair question.

Here's how the process works. All the required steps with retirement plans, life insurance policies, investment accounts, and bank accounts all begin and spring into action only when each institution has received a certified copy of the death certificate. Every blue moon, we are told a death certificate is needed, but it does not have to be a certified copy.

Let's talk about two methods of certifying a death certificate that I have seen a county follow. I will explain the catch that comes with the first type. For decades in the USA, someone in the clerk of court's office or another department of county government would issue death certificates. A county staffer would then take an embossing stamp and squeeze it on the death certificate, creating a physical impression on the paper death certificate sometimes referred to as the seal that contained writing that indicated it was certified.

Suppose the executor or their adviser wanted to send a death certificate to a life insurance company by fax to hasten payment of the death claim because the beneficiary needed funds. The catch was the seal didn't show because the embossing tool didn't contain ink; it only left its physical mark on the certificate. A pencil would be used to delicately shade the embossed seal so that the certificate would be made visible as a certified copy as required by the death claims department. Still, the limitations of an impression left on paper without ink are self-evident.

Some locales have moved away from that procedure, and the paper death certificate has it marked in ink that the death certificate is "certified" so scanning or faxing works smoothly and well, speeding up the payment process for the beneficiary.

Typically, the executor or beneficiary quickly sends a certified copy of the death certificate to each firm that requires it as soon as the family receives them so those institutions have official proof of your loved one's death. The sending of the death certificate is the first vital step to expedite receipt of the deceased's assets. However, as we will see ahead, in some situations, particularly insurance companies recommend a different approach.

Here's the metaphor I use when I teach. Think of the federal and state statutes and IRS regulations as being the bones of the human body, with everyone having the same number of bones. Each retirement plan or firm must obey the laws or regulations relevant to them to remain compliant. In contrast, each plan or company is permitted to "flesh out" that skeletal structure as it prefers. Just as each person looks different, each plan or company develops different policies and procedures. Despite the terrific benefits of beneficiary designations, part of what makes requesting, transferring, or receiving assets of the deceased so cumbersome is that the differing policies of various firms and plans create confusion for the beneficiary or executor. Your savvy awareness can make you more process realistic as well as more patient.

Often, a great place to start to understand the steps required for each institution is on their websites listed under death claims or a similar title. To save you considerable time, cut and paste (or print) a copy of their step-by-step instructions onto as your initial notes for that firm's requirements. Often, one or more steps may not appear completely clear due to the beneficiary's unfamiliarity with the firm's nomenclature or process. Once you have your copy of that institution's steps, call a representative at the firm to walk you through the confusing steps, making notes as needed.

If you use the services of a financial adviser, ask them to work with various plans and firms to retrieve or transfer assets for you. An experienced financial adviser knows what the common obstacles are and can save you many hours of work and lots of headaches. Just because you are the executor or beneficiary doesn't mean you must do each chore yourself. Some forms require your signature and the date; however, having your professional team assist you saves you lots of time and aggravation. Most saliently, completing the forms correctly speeds payment.

Let's go back stage again. As soon as we learn that a client has died, we alert our mothership, and then typically, no monthly checks that the deceased client had been receiving on the day of the month they preferred are sent out any longer. All the "heavy lifting" of moving assets employing various forms that must be filled out in a precise manner does not get underway until we have a death certificate.

Before the death certificate arrives, we check our internal "death matrix," which is a list of steps that may need to be taken based on various circumstances. We are looking for an asset that requires additional processing. By reviewing and preparing, when the death certificate arrives, we are ready to start the process in earnest, to retrieve or transfer assets for beneficiaries, or to move them to their name (ownership) as they prefer.

Typically, it is the beneficiary's (or executor's) responsibility to complete all required tasks so that the institution receives the instructions in proper delivery. Said differently, when the institution completes its processes—usually requiring a death certificate and one of that firm's in-house forms signed and delivered to it— the institution knows it is now empowered to act, based on clear beneficiary or executor instructions, to either cut a check or transfer the deceased's assets.

Utilizing the following action step can help you retain your sanity while completing your goals expeditiously. Suppose you need to reach out to six different institutions that hold assets of the deceased. Set up a separate note page for each institution on a pad of paper, on your laptop, or on the notes section of your phone. It will help organize you. As mentioned above, list the specific steps, often found on that firm's website, which must be taken to retrieve or transfer to the beneficiary the assets or accounts of the deceased as required by each institution. As you complete each requirement or task, check it off as done.

The catch is, sometimes you think you have completed a given requirement, while the institution does not concur. A snag has occurred. Maybe you sent in that company's required form; however, you were unaware the paperwork has been deemed by staff to be incomplete or filled out incorrectly. That means that the company cannot act yet on your instructions.

Invariably, when a snafu occurs, the executor or beneficiary is unaware that some element of the process, which they thought they had completed, is deemed incomplete by one of the institutions. Some firms are prompt at notifying the beneficiary of the outstanding issue; some are slow to do so. You can check with each institution, using a sports metaphor, how far they agree that you have moved the ball down their field toward your goal. Call the firm's staff to ask. Depending on circumstances, we would review how much yardage we have gained in each of six games, or with six institutions, as often as each day, though typically less frequently.

If you are unconvinced of the benefit of creating a separate list for the process of each institution and how many steps currently remain for you to travel, consider this example. You contact institution number 1 to find out what it requires you to do to receive what is now your money. That first institution may be an insurance company, and the second may be a credit union, while the third institution may be a brokerage or securities firm. Those three are such different types of businesses that you can readily see why their policies and requirements may differ so markedly. By making a separate reference sheet for each institution where there are assets to be retrieved or transferred to the beneficiary's name, the unique needs of the different types of companies and plans become more understandable and manageable for you.

Please do not presume because the institution's number 1 and 4 are both insurance companies that their procedures will be the same. I agree they will be similar. However, they each must have their specific requirements satisfied before assets are released or transferred. In summary, ask each of the six businesses, in my example, what steps you must take to achieve your agenda. By jotting down each firm's requirements and keeping track of each level you have completed, you will feel less frazzled and much more in control, and you will achieve your aims sooner.

The Excruciating Sting and Fog of Bereavement

Let's step back from the death certificate and "forms" for a moment to look at the human side of the process. Whether the death occurred suddenly or was long expected, whenever the person dies, the family suffers from the stinging burden of grief. "Michael, my mom had been sick for so long we all thought we were prepared for her death since as time went on, her quality of life declined so much. Though we didn't want to lose her, we didn't want her to suffer. However, when Mom died, we were shocked at how hard her death hit us. We realized that whenever death occurs, one is not prepared." So true.

Once all the immediate activities surrounding the wake and funeral have concluded, I ask the beneficiary to act only at a pace that their grief permits. Some individuals work expeditiously as their activity helps them withstand and better tolerate the depth of their grief, slicing it into smaller, more manageable doses. Having to go to work or, if retired, doing chores can be a blessing to occupy the mind of the individual who is grieving. Work doesn't reduce the feelings of grief; however, needing to complete tasks distracts the bereaved from dwelling nonstop on harrowing feelings of sadness. So many people have shared with me that activity has been therapeutic for them as a distractor.

Suppose an adult child brings the surviving spouse into my office so we can discuss "next steps." Typically, our goal is to assist the widow(er) transferring assets into that surviving spouse's name or ownership "as is," which means without buying or selling any investments. Often, the surviving spouse is accompanied by a loved one (which I heartily encourage), especially during that first month or two after the death of their beloved.

The benefit for the survivor is as they own the assets that were formerly in the name of their spouse, I can reassure them that they have at their fingertips all the assets they need for any expenses over the next two years, which tends to be the most painful and scary stretch of bereavement. It is critical for the financial adviser to do everything they can to reassure the survivor that they have the availability of liquid funds to meet any expenditure so that the bereaved is not needlessly worrying about meeting routine expenses. They likely will be anxious in any case, even ruminating, as that is appropriate behavior considering their tenderness from such a disorienting tragedy. If the family and the adviser work together, they may be able to help reduce the level of anxiety the bereaved widow(er) feels.

The bereavement process is as unique as the individual. Here's an example of what individuals who have lost a spouse have told me: "Michael, though I do not miss my spouse one ounce less, I noticed that for me, at about the two-year mark, I had greater strength to deal with the loss of my husband." Though everyone has their time line until they feel their "greater strength," I have heard about two years length of time quoted several times. If you are going through the painful sting of bereavement, please do not let that time line burden you as your needs may be quite different. Some people fear the depth of their grief at their worst moments will never lessen, and almost always it does.

It is important to note, even in situations where there is no sign of what mental health professionals refer to as complicated grief or bereavement, I have seen bereavement last for a decade or even the remainder of that survivor's life. The survivor may be fully functioning, yet their feelings of profound loss and longing remain.

Abraham and Mary Lincoln suffered the crushing loss of three sons. I read a moving letter of encouragement that Abraham Lincoln wrote to a friend beset with the sharp pains of grief. Lincoln wrote that despite his friend's tragic loss, he would one day be happy again.

In the immediate aftermath of a loss of someone dear—a spouse, a parent, a sibling—typically one of the family members will make at least an initial office visit or at least make a phone call within the first thirty days, often within the first week or two. If they prefer, I visit them at their home. Someone either mails us either one (sometimes two) certified copies of the death certificate or drops them off at our office soon after the family receives them. The type of assets in the accounts enables us to tell the survivor or executor (often the same person) how many death certificates we need to process all the accounts.

The initial postdeath appointment focuses on addressing whatever concerns the survivor has and then transferring assets to the proper ownership of the survivor or beneficiary. It has happened several times that a month or two after the initial meeting, I will receive a phone call from the survivor that goes something like this: "Michael, I remember I came to your office with my son. However, I don't recall what we did. Can you review it with me again?" For many bereaving family members, those first days after their loved one died are a little more than a blur.

Typically, my response is something like this. "To help you have full access to all your assets as soon as possible so that you can be completely confident that you can meet every monthly expense, you signed paperwork instructing us to transfer your deceased spouse's joint account, which you co-owned. At my recommendation and with your permission, we established for you a single-ownership account, so all the funds and assets in your prior joint account have been transferred without cost to you, into your name. On your new account, you are the 100 percent or sole owner. You can access any of the funds in your new individual ownership account whenever you wish. You signed a request to receive a money market checkbook on your new single account, enabling you to write a check whenever you want. At any time, you can call us, and we can instruct the custodian to transfer funds over to your checking account where you bank.

"We also removed your deceased spouse's name as cotrustee on his revocable living trust investment account you have with us, and you now appear on the account as the sole remaining current trustee on your spouse's revocable living trust. (Often, there are several successor trustees as backup).

"Also, we transferred all your husband's traditional IRA and Roth IRA assets into your traditional and Roth IRAs. You are permitted to do this by IRS regs because you are a surviving spouse. As we did this transfer from his traditional and Roth IRAs, you incurred zero tax liability. Now instead of there being two traditional IRAs, his and yours, there is only one traditional IRA. When you receive the month-end statement, it shows the combining of everything from both traditional IRAs into your traditional IRA. Your official investment statement will show the completion of the same process on both your and your husband's Roth IRAs. There is now just in one Roth IRA, in your name, holding all the assets from both your husband's Roth and your Roth IRA combined.

"You also permitted us to help you with the change of beneficiary forms so that as you instructed, your prior contingent beneficiaries are now your primary beneficiaries on both your traditional and Roth IRAs.

"All assets that we assist you with are now in your name and ownership for your comfort and convenience. I recommended, and you agreed, to postpone any investment decisions for as long as possible due to the terrible weight of bereavement. All the assets that were in your joint account and your husband's traditional and Roth IRA were transferred 'as-is,' meaning you continue to retain all assets without any sales occurring. There are still some additional tasks for you on which my team is working. If you'd like, I can ask them to review with you what steps we are taking on your behalf, with your permission that they are completing."

The client's question above is the best evidence for how distorting the intense pain and fog of bereavement can be. It is also the reason why I want someone trusted by the survivor to accompany them to our appointment. Even when an appointment is unrelated to death, I prefer if both spouses visit or a parent and an adult child participate since as the adage goes, "Two heads are better than one." Each party helps the other create questions for me to answer. Also, they help each other understand and remember the content of the meeting, especially anything new or complicated for them.

I have served wealthy people who, during the sharp sting and fog of bereavement, shared concerns if they have enough to meet their expenses. Typically, they would never need to give this a thought. If you are a caregiver, it is beneficial to the person you love if they have available enough assets liquid to reassure them.

When death strikes one partner of a married couple, rapid changes occur to social security and pension check payouts, as well as monthly distributions from IRAs or other accounts. This change in monthly household income may significantly alter what had been, for the couple, predictable incoming cash flow. These changes understandably can be destabilizing and scary for a surviving spouse. Any appropriate reassurance is most helpful.

However, how the caregiver does this is critical. Whisking away their fears dismissively by saying something like, "Mom, stop worrying. You have plenty of money," is frequently an ineffective (though accurate and well-intended) response.

Instead, offer specifics that may prove reassuring: "Mom, would you like me to show you all the assets you currently have available? Would it help comfort you if I contrasted those assets with your monthly expenses? What issues about money concern you the most? Would you like me to get your financial adviser on the phone to discuss this with you? How may I help you? What may I do for you that you may find reassuring?"

Explaining wins; dismissing one's fears as unreasonable may feel belittling and tends not to achieve its aim. By treating the bereaved's worries with genuine respect, the more successful the family member or caregiver will be at mitigating jarring concerns. Listening to their concerns without offering rebuttal may be one hundred times more powerful than telling. Then showing them their liquidity adds to the benefits of attending, lowering their anxiety about bill paying.

Repeating this process several times may mitigate your loved one's fears.

I recommend you consider this approach if you are going through bereavement or you are assisting someone else as their caregiver or executor. Often, it is wise to make only the decisions necessary when they need deciding. I try to put as few tasks on the survivor's plate as possible. Why? To be considerate and also to prevent them from making an error over a decision that can wait until they can feel and think more like themselves. Bereavement creates the risk of decision-making blind spots and intense emotions; particularly fear and anxiety may cause outsized, irreversible errors by the surviving spouse.

I recommend to clients that they make no major decisions that are not necessary for two years. When they are struggling with a decision that may be impacted by feelings of grief, I share with them examples of what I have seen through the eyes of others. Some of the experiences I learned about or witnessed were positive, while others were negative. I see it as vital to the widow(er) that I present a spectrum of outcomes for the bereaved client to consider as part of their decision-making process, not solely the "good" or the "bad."

"I Hate Forms, but They Are so Necessary"

Let's return to the topic of forms. Oh, joy! As a refresher, I previously mentioned death certificates and forms. Why? Assets of the deceased may be in several retirement plans and at various insurance or financial institutions. The beneficiary may either prefer their portion of the deceased's assets be retrieved or distributed for them to have funds to spend.

What are the most common expenditures of beneficiaries with the funds they have received from the deceased during the first two years? Paying off debt, purchasing autos, traveling, upgrading their home, paying tuition for their children's education, boosting the size of their money market emergency fund, and reinvesting in different vehicles better suited to their needs are most common.

For the portion of the deceased's assets that the beneficiary receives that they choose not to distribute to spend, the recipient may want to transfer those assets into their name. This next point is crucial. Astutely, the beneficiary may wish to avoid being taxed now on the receipt of some of Mom's (or Dad's) tax-deferred accounts, so this may inhibit how much they elect to distribute for spending in each tax year.

That first year after the owner's death, the beneficiary may want to take a sizable distribution of some of the assets transferring to their name or ownership. Doing so often will trigger a painful tax bite. However, by maintaining the tax-deferred status on a large portion of account or plan assets they received, the beneficiary may be able to grow those assets while taking out reasonably sized distributions each year, or as needed or wanted. When possible, the goal is not to distribute such large amounts that the beneficiary feels like Uncle Sam is getting too much of their newly received assets.

Another vital distinction is that transferring and distributing assets have different implications. To make these distinctions clear, let's start with the most straightforward example, which is related to insurance company "forms" (paperwork).

Suppose your spouse has died or you are an adult child assisting a surviving parent in the immediate aftermath of the death of their spouse. First, for our purposes, let's class their insurance-related forms into only two hemispheres: life insurance and annuity forms. As life insurance forms are much more accessible, let's start there for clarity.

Suppose that you are the beneficiary of someone's life insurance policy. You may be the sole beneficiary or you may be, for example, one of six recipients who will receive death benefit proceeds from the life insurance policy. Life insurance death claims forms tend to be much less complicated than annuity insurance company death claims forms.

Often the top box under payout options is your request to have a check for the total proceeds of the life insurance policy. By far, this is what most individuals select. I give high marks to life insurance companies as I have found them to be quick payers of death proceeds. Typically, I recommend to my clients that we start there first so that significant sums of money can arrive speedily to the beneficiary who often is an executor. Having liquid funds available reduces anxiety for the family as they can readily meet any surprises they encounter. As they are trying to settle the estate of the deceased, the first considerable expense often is the funeral bill unless they prepaid their funeral.

Some insurance company death claims payouts transfer into a money market account of the insurer. The beneficiary then doesn't receive a check for total proceeds. Instead, what they receive is a thin money market checkbook with about six checks from which the beneficiary of the life insurance policy can withdraw the funds as they need it.

I understand the desire of some insurance companies to continue to earn some profit on the death claim payout via their money market. After all, the bereaved may be struggling so much with the horrible pains of grief and overwhelmed by the many chores that settling an estate bring so that they may leave some or all the funds for an extended period in that new money market established by the insurer.

At times, it seemed some death claims proceeds went into the money market as a routine procedure. One rationalization is that the beneficiary did earn interest on their death claim payout. I prefer if the beneficiary wants the insurer's money market that they affirmatively select that option. I have found that if a check is mailed directly to the recipient to deposit locally, the tactile and visual receipt of having a sizable cashable check in their hands is more comforting and reassuring to them than being surprised by a money market checkbook that they don't recall requesting.

Though the dollar amount of the death claim's payment the beneficiary receives is identical in either case, I have noticed some approaches psychologically soothe the bereaved more than others. I have found a check in the beneficiary's hands that arrives promptly produces the maximum relief from financial worry. Then the recipient decides to which institution they prefer to bring their funds. Often, those checks are deposited at their local bank in the client's checking or money market account to meet expenses that are a by-product of a loved one's death.

Please note, in some insurance company vehicles, particularly annuities, there are a multitude of payout or distribution choices that can be selected by a beneficiary. This myriad of choices can prove quite confusing and intimidating. How do they sort through those options? They can get necessary information about the policy and its various payout options from the death claims department of the insurance company although typically not advice or strategies from the staff of the death claims department.

Your insurance professional or your financial adviser typically are excellent resources for reviewing the pros and cons of each option. Whether the given vehicle was acquired through us or not, I assist in figuring out, based on listening to the beneficiary's needs, what may fit them the best. After considering the various payout options, the recipient chooses whatever they decide is best.

One crucial variable, the internal rules of some insurance companies, may require that if an annuity has multiple beneficiaries, all beneficiaries must make the same "election." All six recipients, in my example, must make an identical choice no matter their individual needs or preferences. As you'll see below, this inflexibility is often not as bad as it may seem at first blush. In this hypothetical, that happens to be the rules of that insurance company. Please note, all "annuity" companies are insurance companies.

Some insurance companies permit each of their annuity policy beneficiaries to independently select any of the options for payout available without concern for what other recipients of the same policy choose to do. I prefer this feature for beneficiaries. However, since there is a high likelihood that the beneficiaries may all request a lump-sum payout since it is the payout option so frequently chosen, those companies who required uniformity of choice of all recipients tend not to disadvantage the beneficiaries by their rule, in many cases.

Let's return to the certified copy of the death certificate and various institutional forms that the beneficiary is required to fill out to retrieve or transfer the assets they are receiving from the deceased's plan or account. Both a death certificate and whatever that company's or retirement plan's required forms are, that when the beneficiary has completed and signed and dated them, must be received by the processing centers (the back offices) of those institutions. The death certificate assures the institution that the individual has died, and the institution's forms, which are of their design, let the company or the retirement plan know what the beneficiary is instructing that institution to do with the deceased's assets to which the beneficiary is entitled. These instructions are critical.

It is essential that the beneficiary fill out the forms correctly. Mistakes beneficiaries make when they do some unfamiliar tasks themselves can be costly to them. We ask the recipients or executors to allow us to complete their forms to prevent them from accidentally selecting a choice that is less than optimum. Then we explain how each section of the institutions' required forms benefits the beneficiary. After we fill out the forms, we ask the client to review our work to be sure that is what they prefer done with their new assets.

My preference to get the distribution or transferring process started is to send out the death certificates to the various institutions ASAP. Alternatively, when talking with some death claims department staff on numerous occasions dealing with many firms, I have been advised to wait until the required forms are completed and to send both the death certificate and the forms in simultaneously so the two are not separated. If you send the death certificate long before sending in the required forms, to officially notify the firm, do not be surprised if the firm asks you later to resend the death certificate. Many times, when there are multiple beneficiaries, I have received the insurer's advice that if it is not inconvenient for the recipients, have all their forms sent together along with the death certificate to prevent the need to resend forms.

Otherwise, the beneficiary may believe all the required documents have been received and they are merely waiting for their check, which presumably should be arriving shortly. Meanwhile, that firm thinks one of its requirements remains outstanding. Sometimes, after sending everything required, if they came separately, that firm's imaging system may not have connected various documents, so it doesn't register with the software that the firm has all it requires for payment or transfer.

The beneficiary may have sent the death certificate to the firm three weeks ago. Then the firm's required form requesting a check for the life insurance death benefit may have been sent by the beneficiary eight days later. However, the firm is not aware it has both required items because of some snag that occurred since the document and form arrived on different days. Meanwhile, the beneficiary is waiting for payment. The firm is waiting to receive whatever is ostensibly "missing" that is needed to complete the process so that it can cut the check. Neither waiting party may be communicating with the other, so both are in the dark!

Often, the firm doesn't contact the beneficiary that something is missing, according to its incorrect understanding. The firm is going to wait patiently for what it needs from the beneficiary, who may be dealing with grief and who has other more salient tasks to complete while being paid each day on the assets under management. I have found death claims departments to be excellent at setting reasonable expectations for the timing of the arrival of the amount of the check. Payout often occurs ten days to two weeks after all forms have been received and reviewed. Please ask the staff when you are due to receive the check at your home. I have found firms often get the check to the beneficiary in less time than the stated window, striving to underpromise and overdeliver, which is terrific.

What usually leads to the identification of the snag? After waiting for check processing, the beneficiary or their insurance or financial adviser checks with the death claims or operations department of the insurer, discovering the cause of the unexpected delay. This inquiry leads to the discovery that the firm cannot find something that the beneficiary(ies) or executor sent. Often, documents must be resent to the firm by the beneficiary or their adviser to complete the process for the beneficiary to receive payment. By doing so, if you don't receive your expected payout, it lets you know to call to see if there is a snag.

While some companies may require both the death certificate and their in-house forms to be completed and mailed to that company's processing center, today, many firms accept the faxing or scanning of the documents and forms that the firm requests. Every firm's requirements differ.

To protect the security of the information, faxing has proven secure, and encrypting emails with standard 256-bit encryption has also been very successful, though the firm may have its preferred method of encryption. If you do not encrypt, a scanned email may be vulnerable.

However, do not ignore the success rate of the USPS. For more than thirty-five years, I have received and sent out every type of form, document, and check without any security breach. I think the US postal service is terrific based on both my business and personal experience. At times, we receive seven-figure checks in the mail, and except for an occasional delay if a sack of mail is misplaced, USPS delivery has been as secure for our clients and us as any other means they or we have utilized.

Impressive too is overnight mail because of its speed and especially for its tracking number; however, be aware that nearly always the receiving firms have one address for regular correspondence and a different address for overnight or express mail. If you need to receive death proceeds speedily, you can request that the insurance company send your check by an overnight delivery service with the insurer charging only a nominal amount to you, which is subtracted from the death proceeds (for example, −$25).

You can have your investment or insurance professional advise you on what route may be best for you or your loved one regarding asset distributions or transfers while being aware and wary of potential tax consequences. I will explain what we do as an example, so if you find this useful, you can ask your adviser to help you similarly.

If there is another company involved, that is, if a different custodian holds those assets than where our clients' assets are under custody, I request the beneficiary come to my office bringing any monthly or quarterly statements about the insurance or retirement plan that I do not have available. My purpose is to talk to the representative of the plan or insurer, asking a series of illuminating questions that I know to ask that the surviving spouse, beneficiary, executor, or adult child may not know to ask of that institution.

Using the speaker option on my phone lets the beneficiary hear for themselves the agent's answer to every question that I asked. It is an interactive conversation. I do not know in advance all the detours I may need to take during the phone call. I invite the beneficiary to ask any question at any time. In one thirty-minute phone call, often, both the intended recipient and I have been updated on all the crucial aspects of the plan, policy, or account assets held elsewhere.

My questions are designed to sort through options for the beneficiary as well as potential tax liabilities and other pitfalls. The beneficiary can hear and "see" how I am thinking about the process for them. We both learn a lot about the nuances of that institution's internal policies.

I am particularly concerned about fees and penalties for the beneficiary. Also, this is salient to be aware of; there may be a window of time during which the beneficiary may select their preferred option without fees or penalties. However, after that period window has closed, sometimes within ninety days or less, any distribution or transfer instructions received after the cutoff then trigger fees or penalties. The answers I receive from each institution on time windows and costs impact the route I recommend the beneficiary take after both of us finish sifting through the pros and cons of each option.

With my phone on speaker, I dial the company that has some of the assets that the deceased left using the beneficiary clause and designation to speak with the beneficiary, who is sitting in my office. After inputting whatever data the computer voice requires as identifiers, eventually, the recipient and I can hear a company representative join our call.

I introduce myself, my occupation, and my role. "Hi! I am Michael Wittenberg. I am a financial adviser for [the name of the firm]. I am serving as an adviser to the beneficiary of this account [or plan] that is in the name or ownership of _____, who is now deceased." I continue with, "The beneficiary is with me and will give you permission to speak with me, and the beneficiary understands that you will first have to ask them several security questions to be sure they are whom they claim."

The representative then asks several security questions of the beneficiary, which may include their full name, address, and the address of the deceased, after which they will ask the beneficiary if the beneficiary permits them to speak to me as well as to give me any account information. One "catch" of these calls is that the permission the beneficiary provides to the agent regarding my participation lasts only for the duration of that call. If I think of something else later and the beneficiary is no longer in my office, if the question is specific to that deceased's assets and not generic, a subsequent representative appropriately will not provide me with any account information adhering to sound required confidentiality procedures.

Which types of institutions am I calling on behalf of the executor or beneficiary? Typically, I am reaching out to the representative of a life insurance company, the insurance company that had sold the deceased an annuity, or of the investment house that the 401(k) plan sponsor—the employer—selected to handle all the myriad issues of the 401(k), which the employer wisely farms out. I may be calling a bank, credit union, savings and loan, or other firms offering IRAs, for example.

It is not uncommon that after I have ended the call, as we are considering what we have just learned, either the beneficiary or I think of another question we hadn't thought to ask in the prior call. I call that institution back again, and invariably, a different agent for that firm is on our follow-up call. With the beneficiary on speaker, I not only ask that specific additional question but also review whatever I think are the most pertinent answers we have received from the first representative with that next agent.

Though I am expecting the answers from the second agent to confirm what the first representative indicated, sometimes, though not too often, we receive a discrepant reply. When that occurs, I will explain that I have called twice, that I received divergent answers, that I mean no disrespect to the agent currently on the phone, and that they indeed may be correct. However, I would like to speak directly to a supervisor to get their insight on the correct answer to the question. If they say, "I will put you on hold and ask the supervisor," I request they let me speak directly to the supervisor. They could have me on hold and not want to ask their supervisor in case their error or lack of knowledge could reflect poorly on them. Instead, they ask a coworker in another cubicle whom they think is knowledgeable. I prefer the answer to come from the horse's mouth.

Here's the most common situation where, though I typically prefer the death certificate and company forms to be returned together to avoid confusion and a need to resend it all, I instead decide to send just the death certificate off quickly. To protect confidentiality, which is essential to all institutions, suppose I reprise most of the call process that I explained above. However, when I call the company representative of the plan or insurer and inform them I have the surviving spouse, executor, or beneficiary on speaker with me, their first step is to see if they have an image of the deceased's death certificate in their software system.

When the representative does not see the listing of the account owner as deceased on their computer monitor, they are not allowed to tell us a single specific, which is appropriate. (The representative doesn't know if we are scamsters trying to wheedle account info about the owner improperly.) In that case, I continue with, "Since I am in your profession, I understand you may not disclose any account information whatsoever. The purpose of my call is solely to ask general questions about this type of product or account so that we are both sure of the standard options available and to request, if permissible, that you send a set of their forms to the home of the deceased."

Sometimes, the representative will do the latter. Nearly always, they typically will explain the former generically, which gives us a head start on our mulling over the pros and cons of each option. If they don't send the forms to the address of the deceased, I fax off a copy of the death certificate. Then a few days later, in a subsequent phone call, the death certificate shows on the rep's software system, so they know our call is legit.

Then I request the following: "If your firm hasn't already put into the mail to the address of the deceased your company's required forms for distributing or transferring assets into the name of the beneficiary, please do so. I request that you email a duplicate set of those same forms to my email address as the adviser and the email address of the beneficiary." I then provide both email addresses to the representative.

Often, the representative needs to ask the permission of the beneficiary if the rep may email me the forms the firm is sending to the address of the deceased (the only official address on record at that firm). Often, the policy of firms is to mail one set of requested forms to the address of the account owner, despite notification that the account or plan owner is deceased, as a security safeguard.

Once the beneficiary gives the representative permission, often while the intended recipient is still in my office, the email with the required forms for distribution or transfer arrives via my company email. I print out two copies of the attachment containing the forms. Then the beneficiary and I review them to see in print the options we were discussing by phone. This review of possibilities and forms accelerates the payout process dramatically.

So often, no one helps the beneficiary, especially if they had nothing to do with selling the deceased that asset. Making those calls performs a vital service to the surviving spouse, executor, adult child, and beneficiary. My view is that like any financial adviser, unfortunately, I cannot make stock markets rise; however, I can provide responsive service.

Transfers or Rollovers

What I tell the individuals and families I have the privilege to serve is if you are satisfied with your company-sponsored retirement plan, typically there's no need to act under the adage, "If it ain't broke, don't fix it." Does it meet your current needs? What are its costs to you? Are you knowledgeable about investing, the economy, and markets? Would you like the help of an advisor on this sizable percentage of your net worth? Do you have emerging additional requirements or preferences that your plan doesn't address? I would start with those question for your deliberations.

Company-sponsored plans have available to them what is known as a "safe harbor" if they only provide their retirement plan participants with education and do not provide advice. The limitations of the safe harbor frustrate many plan participants who joke with me that previously they "threw darts" as to what to select as the investment options in their 401(k), for example. They readily indicate they didn't understand what was prudent for them to choose among the investment choices their plan makes available. What mix of assets and at what percentages were right for their risk tolerance or their long-term objectives? They didn't know, and in fairness, that's not their field. Meanwhile, the stakes for plan participants are so high, and their needs often go unmet.

What I have found is their company-sponsored retirement plan sometimes feels like a black box mystery to some plan participants. They wish their employer would do more to help them. I understand their frustration. If I were the company, I would rigidly adhere to the "education only" safe harbor, or else the liabilities could be immense. However, that still leaves the employee "stuck" without the assistance and guidance they reasonably crave.

It's purely my viewpoint, while I think it is essential for employers to be offered a safe harbor by regulators, which they overwhelmingly, nearly universally adopted, I believe the safe harbor could be designed differently so that the employer does not take on unneeded and unwanted liability. And the plan participant may receive sound investment advice. It need not be "either-or." It can be "both," with regulatory changes. However, I am cognizant of the terrain that plan participants find themselves in, which is not the terrain on which I prefer they would be traveling.

Plan participants who have spent many years building significant assets sometimes need and seek professional guidance, especially since defined benefit retirement plans, those excellent old-style monthly check plans for retirees, started to vanish in the 1990s.

Despite their many benefits, there are problematic limitations with defined contribution plans (403(b)s and 401(k)s, for example), which recent legislation has attempted to address. It is my opinion, despite some modest improvements, plan participants need additional assistance without harming their employers, who may stop offering their 401(k) if suddenly their liabilities grew.

Keep in mind that employers take on all the headaches of bringing in an outside plan sponsor because the government offers the employer an inducement. Employers receive a corporate tax deduction for their matching contributions (if they choose to match) and for your contributions, making the difficulties of offering a defined contribution retirement plan worth the aggravation of employee grumbling during inevitable recessions. Any time management spending focused on their company-sponsored plan, this takes valuable time away from their core mission: running the company profitably. The plan, while useful to attract and retain employees, is scarcely any different than their archrival's 401(k). So often, it does not net the employer a specific edge for employee recruitment and retention while being a distraction for management.

Plan participants may be motivated to make changes, such as partial or lump-sum distributions and transfers to traditional IRAs for a variety of reasons. Often, their retirement plan balance has grown significantly over the years, so they seek professional guidance. If you involve an adviser, you are likely to pay considerably higher costs. Some individuals seek more investment choices than 401(k) offers. Also, the individual may want additional help with monthly income distributions as they retire.

Let's suppose for you or the person you love, the prudent action to be taken is to transfer or roll over assets from your company-sponsored retirement plan, such as a 401(k), to a traditional IRA. How may you do this successfully? I am defining success as you transfer all the assets you have in your 401(k) (called taking a lump-sum distribution) without triggering any current-year tax liability as you move your funds to a traditional IRA. It is essential that you retain the tax-deferred status of all the plan assets as you transfer funds to your IRA. With care, this is achievable. (Sometimes, such an asset move is referred to as a rollover. However, a rollover is a general term, used loosely, when more technically, the term *institutional transfer of assets* may be more accurate). Whenever possible, it is best if the assets are sent from one institution to another institution so that the process is considered as a transfer, not as a rollover.

To answer this transfer question well, I will explain how a generic transfer of any accounts or investments typically occurs in the investment world, and then I will return specifically to transfers of company-sponsored plans like 401(k)s. Often in the investment world, whatever firm is receiving the client's assets does all the paperwork. Suppose you have a joint-ownership account at a brokerage firm and you want it transferred to a rival firm. The receiving firm would ask you for a copy of your latest statement. Your account statement provides the receiving firm an accurate "picture" of the assets they are transferring for you to it. The receiving firm fills out transfer paperwork, which you sign and date, and it's your signature that empowers the receiving firm to instruct the firm where your assets are currently held to release and transfer your assets as you have indicated on the transfer form.

Be transparent with your adviser regarding any investments you currently own that you wish not to have sold (which in some accounts could trigger significant capital gains taxes) so they transfer "as-is," which means no asset sales occur. You select, or your adviser may recommend which assets they think is best for you to move "as is" and which assets may be sold at the other firm before the transfer occurs. Often, your adviser may want all assets to be transferred "as is" to make the transfer as smooth and quick as possible. Once your assets arrive at the new firm, then your adviser may implement the changes to which you agree. With this background as a general guideline, let's look at typical procedures for transferring your 401(k) to a traditional IRA.

The process to transfer a company-sponsored retirement plan varies from plan to plan based on the preferences of the employer. Here's the most common method used, but your retirement plan may have different policies and procedures. Typically, each company-sponsored retirement plan has its own set of forms that must be completed to effect a partial or lump-sum distribution from that plan. I prefer that our clients let us fill out these forms for them to prevent an error as well as to make the process easier for them. To ship funds as an institution-to-institution transfer, which often is best, you or your loved one need the name of the custodian who will hold your assets in the traditional IRA.

Here's how the retirement plan distribution check from the 401(k) or another type of plan may read: the name of the custodian or custodial firm is at the start of the "Make payable to." The custodial institution is responsible for holding your assets. I was studying two custodial firms sometime ago, and at that juncture, these two archrivals each held more than $33 trillion in assets!

Let's say you are transferring your assets to custodian XYZ. Then either of two terms follows the name of the custodian, and both are fine: FBO is "for the benefit of," or C/F is "custodian for," and then your name is typed in the remainder of the "Make this check payable to" line. It would look like this: "Make the check payable to: XYZ custodian for the benefit of you or your loved one." How does this plating of the check help you?

Even though this is your money, you cannot cash the check as it is made out to an institution that has the responsibility to hold your assets for you (for which the custodian is paid a fee often by the investment firm at which you have established your traditional IRA). The advantage is the way this check is cut means it is leaving the institution holding your 401(k) assets and moving directly to another institution on your behalf. Even if your check was written this way for you and was mailed to your home for you to either walk it over or to send it to the local office of the firm you have established your traditional IRA at to receive these funds, it remains an institution-to-institution transfer of your money, which is best.

The receiving firm hands you or mails you a receipt for the check, after which it holds your assets at the custodian of the receiving firm. Please then review your next official monthly statement, which will indicate the posting date of your funds.

There's a firewall to protect you. Whether your assets are in your 401(k) or your traditional IRA, a custodian for each must hold these assets to protect you. Your funds and assets do not commingle with your adviser's or your adviser's firm's assets. Your retirement plan money is not to mix with your employer's assets, and whatever the firm provides your employer with its version of a 401(k), that company cannot commingle your assets with its assets. This safeguard lets you, your adviser, your adviser's firm, and everyone who works with these assets sleep at night. You may hear the term *custodial bank*. That firm is responsible for holding your assets, and a custodial institution is unlike a commercial bank where you may have a checking and money market account; it may own a separate unit to act as custodian for securities-related assets.

Now let's travel to issues related to the transferring of retirement account assets to beneficiaries. If you are the spousal beneficiary of your deceased spouse's 401(k), you can transfer the pretax portion of those assets into your traditional IRA in an institution-to-institution transfer, maintaining full tax deferral in the transfer process. Thus, your deceased spouse's IRA or other pretax retirement plan assets typically can be merged into your traditional IRA.

The area to be careful is if you are a nonspousal beneficiary— usually the adult child of a deceased parent's retirement plan, such as a 403(b) or 401(k), for example, or a traditional or Roth IRA that your deceased parent owned. Unless the amount of money involved that you will receive is small, in which case you may need the funds and be willing to pay tax on any pretax distributions, typically, I help the beneficiary set up what is referred to by various names: a conduit IRA, an inherited IRA, or a beneficiary IRA.

If you find yourself in this position, receiving tax-deferred assets either as a primary or contingent beneficiary, remember to be careful about the following issues. Under emerging legislation still working its way through Congress as I write this, the age for RMDs—required minimum distributions—is in the year one reaches age 70.5 (though there is an exception). If the legislation passes in the form it did in the House of Representatives; the RMD age is expected to increase to age 72.

If you are the nonspousal beneficiary of a 401(k) or traditional IRA, it is critical to determine whether the deceased completed their RMD distribution for the year in the year they died. If they did not, typically, before the beneficiary transfers the deceased's traditional or company-sponsored plan assets into the beneficiary IRA of the nonspouse, they must distribute the amount that the deceased was due to take out to fulfill that year's RMD. Frequently, that distribution is placed in the estate checking account for bill paying as the estate is being settled.

Second, by December 31 of the year *after* the plan or IRA owner died, as you are a nonspousal beneficiary, you must begin taking your RMD distributions on the beneficiary or inherited IRA that you established. Under the new legislation that is being worked on as I finish this work, the distribution schedule for beneficiary IRAs is being accelerated to only a ten-year payout schedule, which means you must distribute all the tax-deferred assets, if you go at the slowest pace, in just ten years, which is a much shorter time window. The US Senate's preferred version was a five-year distribution schedule, not a more generous ten-year payout scheme.

If you are a nonspousal beneficiary of, for example, your recently deceased parent's traditional IRA or Roth IRA, you *must* keep those beneficiary IRA assets separate from any IRAs you may have established for yourself. You are *not* permitted to roll over or transfer the beneficiary IRA assets to any personal IRAs that you may have created for yourself.

Be sure each year, starting in the year after the deceased IRA account owner's death, that you distribute at least the RMD amount. You can always distribute more if you wish. On any pretax distributions, be keenly aware of the tax consequences as your distribution amount adds to, and thus impacts, your overall income for that tax year. See your tax and investment adviser to discuss various strategies to minimize your tax burden while taking distributions that serve you well.

"Shield My Money from the Taxman! The Joys of Tax Deferral!"

Tax deferral means that while the owner's assets are in a 401(k) and a traditional IRA, without any distributions occurring, there is no current taxation on those assets or accounts. If an individual takes no distributions from their retirement plan (informally, if the account owner does not withdraw money or assets from their company-sponsored or personal retirement plans), the owner is not currently taxed on any assets they own in the retirement plan. This tax deferral can last for decades. You can easily imagine the opportunity for capital to grow when federal and state governments refrain from taxing various retirement accounts year after year.

Let's visualize a rectangular box with the top open and you are looking into your receptacle. Into your first box, please suppose you have put in thin cardboard dividers that leave you with ten compartments. You can picture this as even-sized compartments if you wish or, better yet, as uneven amounts of space for each compartment. Now suppose that original box represents your 401(k) (or the 401(k) of the deceased). Next, you have or own a second rectangular box that is smaller. In it, you place dividers that produce five compartments. Suppose this second box represents your (or the deceased's) traditional IRA.

In each compartment, you have an investment. For illustration, it might be an investment of the common stock of giant domestic companies, while in the other chambers in your retirement plans, you may be investing in short-term and intermediate-term US government and corporate bond. As an example, suppose one compartment holds utility stocks. These are just a few possible investment vehicles a given investor may have in their retirement accounts.

You can track the value and performance of your accounts by either logging online or by reading (or at least attempting to decipher) your monthly or quarterly official statements of those two boxes or retirement accounts. Many investors like to see the overall market value of their accounts, the total amount that they have in each of their boxes, as well as the current market value of each investment in its discrete compartment within their retirement accounts.

If we look in each compartment, what we may see is that some of the investments your two accounts (401(k) and traditional IRA) held may have paid a dividend, usually received quarterly into the retirement accounts. Some investments you own inside a given compartment may have paid interest to your accounts.

Let's suppose you own a 401(k) worth $500K and a traditional IRA worth $100K. In this hypothetical, twelve months passes; and during that year, markets are quite bullish, that is, rising sharply, with the strength of a bull. The value of your 401(k) increases by +$50K over twelve months, so now its total current market value is $550K, up +10 percent for the year. The traditional IRA rises by +$12K, so its rate of return for twelve months clocks in at +12 percent in this metaphor, and the traditional IRA's current market account value is +$112K.

How much additional income tax did you pay during that taxable year when your employer-sponsored retirement account increased in value by +$50K and your personal traditional IRA increased by +$12K? Your total increase in the market value of those two retirement accounts is +$ 62k! If you do not take any funds out of either account, that is, if you do not make a distribution from either account, you pay zero additional in income tax on your impressive market performance. Why?

Those two types of retirement accounts are tax-deferred. Until you take funds out of either or both, said more precisely, until you make a distribution, you pay no federal income tax on those two retirement accounts as well as no state income taxes. You are not required to pay ordinary income tax to the federal government on that additional amount you accumulated for retirement in those accounts while those funds remain in your accounts. Also, typically, you pay no state income taxes, in those states that have them, on any increase in the value of your retirement accounts if you do not take any funds out of your retirement accounts that year. Only when you distribute funds from these two boxes or retirement accounts do you pay income taxes (typically fed and often state taxes, but not in all states, depends on your state of domicile).

Let's return to those accounts or rectangular boxes. Think of the outer wall of the box protecting you or shielding out the government. See it as the account structure that "walls out" the government from taxing you then. The outer wall of the boxes prevents the government from taking some of your accounts' profits or principal, provided you withdrew no assets from those two boxes during each year.

Also, you may have seen in a given year a substantial growth in the principal amount of one or more of your investments within your two retirement accounts. You may choose to sell several of your investment holdings in some of the compartments that grew substantially. If you follow this strategy, you would harvest that profit and "rebalance" or move those gains that you reaped by selling inside your 401(k) and traditional IRA. You could redirect some of your retirement plan profits to other investment choices that you consider worth purchasing because you find them to be at attractive valuations currently.

For the next part of this hypothetical example, suppose that of the +$62K combined increase in your 401(k) and traditional IRA, 100 percent of that twelve-month increase was only the result of capital appreciation (growth). Let's pretend you did not receive any interest or dividends and all your gains in your two retirement accounts hail solely from you enjoying that the market prices of some of your assets rose in value to the tune of a combined +$62K and then you sell those assets.

If you buy an asset like 1,000 shares of company stock LMNOP at $10 per share, for a total of $10K and you sell that same stock at $14 per share, $14 × 1,000 shares equals $14K, so you saw an increase in your investment capital by +$4K. Suppose that +$4K was just one of the investments you had purchased in your traditional IRA, so that explains +$4K of the +$62K in profit of your two retirement accounts during that robust market year.

If you sold the stock inside your traditional IRA and rebalanced your holdings, you harvested the increase in your capital (along with the original amount of equity you invested in that stock) and you reinvested your money into some other investment within your traditional IRA. Besides income tax, you may be familiar with a tax obligation referred to as a capital gain tax. The benefit of tax deferral is that it shields your dividends, interest, and growth from current taxation. Tax deferral also prevents the application of capital gains taxes from taking any of your +$4K for the federal government and state tax collectors.

So as I mentioned in the hypothetical, if all +$62K in the increase of the two retirement account values, how much of your +$62K would be subject to capital gains taxes? Again, the answer is a delightful zero! The tax-deferred character of your two retirement accounts prevented you from paying any income or capital gains taxes on any of the +$ 62K, whether it was all from growth in market value or much more likely from a mix of dividends, interest, and price appreciation of your retirement investments.

Year after year, if you do not elect to take a distribution from your retirement accounts, you avoid paying taxes on the funds within them. As is evident, tax deferral is an incredibly powerful advantage for any investor accumulating assets in preparation for retirement, and it remains so beneficial even after the individual has retired.

Here's another important distinction: if you had owned the identical investments outside your two tax-deferred accounts, what may have been the tax consequences to you? Suppose you had the equal number of shares of the same investments held in a single- or joint-ownership account or a revocable living trust account, as you did inside your 401(k) and traditional IRA. If you harvested all the +$62K in profit, would you have to pay federal and possibly state income tax on your considerable gains? Single- and joint-ownership accounts, as well as revocable living trust accounts, are not tax-deferred accounts like retirement accounts. Therefore, you may owe significant capital gains taxes, whereas in your retirement accounts, you can use that interest earned—those dividends paid—and that growth of capital would be additional capital available to invest in increasing your retirement assets.

Let's look at an example in a year where the stock market falls. To simplify the model, whether a loss occurred in your 401(k) or a traditional IRA, for example, let's pretend that your holdings decline sharply, so you sell some of the assets that you have in your 401(k). In our hypothetical, suppose that you experience a capital loss of −$50K in a bruising market. Does Uncle Sam allow you to write off that −$50K as a sweet tax deduction on your losses? No! Why not? If Uncle Sam doesn't get to tax your capital gains when you sell at a significant profit—up +$62K in our earlier hypothetical—they are not going to allow you to make government eat a capital loss, giving you an excellent way to reduce your tax owed that year as filed via your Form 1040. There are neither capital gains or losses applied to tax-deferred plans, such as 401(k)s and traditional and Roth IRAs. Why not? Because back to my metaphor of the box, Uncle Sam, thankfully, is shielded out. The "outer wall" of the retirement plan prevents the federal and state governments from receiving any tax revenue from your activity within your company and personal retirement plans (such as a 403(b) and IRAs of all types).

When does the government finally get to tax your retirement plans, both employer-sponsored and your retirement plans? Only when you elect to distribute funds from your plans. However, then you are not taxed at what may be, for you, a lower capital gains tax rate; you pay taxes at ordinary income tax rates.

If you do take out any retirement account distributions, you will pay taxes on that amount that exits your retirement plan(s). If you take the funds before 59.5 years of age, in addition to paying taxes, it is possible that you may pay a 10 percent penalty in addition to ordinary income tax rates on your distribution, though there are some sensible exceptions to the penalties that the IRS allows. Fortunately, today, many exceptions enable individuals to take a distribution from their IRAs before age 59.5, helping them avoid the 10 percent penalty, though they still must pay income taxes at ordinary (regular) federal income rates on the dollar amount distributed.

"What tax rate will I pay on my IRA distribution?" Concern about the taxes owed to the federal government and some state taxing authorities is a frequent and an astute question, the answer to which influences how large an amount of dollars or assets an individual may choose to distribute from their retirement plans in a given tax year. The answer is not a set percentage rate or set dollar amount. It depends on whether the dollar amount of your distribution leaves you still in the highest tax bracket into which you have crossed. Alternatively, did you take out so large a distribution that now some of the retirement assets or dollars distributed, when added to all your other taxable income for the year, bump you up into a new, even higher tax bracket?

The top tax bracket that an individual or a couple reaches in a given tax year is called their marginal tax rate. Think of that as being the highest percentage rate of federal tax you currently pay. Before you take a retirement plan distribution, it is wise to look at a current year tax bracket federal tax chart and match your current income for the year to that chart. What is the highest federal tax bracket your last dollars earned?

Said differently, when you match your ordinary income to the chart, what is your highest bracket? Then roughly calculate how much wiggle room remains in your current top tax bracket without you crossing into an even higher bracket or to a new marginal tax rate.

Let's say you are in the 24 percent federal tax bracket for 2019, and that is your marginal tax rate, which means none of your income is taxed higher than 24 percent. That is, 24 percent is your current top tax bracket this tax year. If you distributed $10K, you may happen to remain in your current marginal tax rate, meaning you would pay the same 24 percent tax rate on that $10K from your retirement plan. If you took out a distribution of $50K, you might be deep enough into the 24 percent tax bracket already that now you push above into the next tax bracket, which as of this writing is the 32 percent tax bracket. That may mean that on some of the $50K retirement plan distribution, you may owe the federal government 32 percent!

You can see why I urge my clients to view any money that they take out of their retirement plans in a given year as the last dollars they earned, meaning they are their most costly dollars. Using that metaphor of the individual's retirement distribution being their most expensive or highest income earned in a year (at ordinary income tax rates, no less) makes taxpayers more attuned to distribute what they need only.

In the example above, instead of Uncle Sam getting 24 percent of that individual's retirement distribution, some of that individual's money is now dinged at 32 percent, a much higher marginal federal tax rate. Talk with your tax and investment professionals about how to optimize your distributions so that you have what you need while limiting the federal government's tax bite.

Sometimes, I can help clients with the following approach. The client calls or visits me in October. The clients want −$70K to be distributed from one retirement plan that for them, let's suppose, is an entirely taxable distribution. Ouch! I suggest that the client or I talk to their tax adviser to determine if there is value for them in following this strategy. If the client does not have to have the entire $70K distributed immediately, where the whole $70K is reported in one tax year, how much is best for the client to distribute this tax year, and how much is to be distributed the first week of January in the new tax year? We can calculate approximately the tax savings if the client uses two years to shoulder the burden of the tax bite rather than just one year, possibly hurting them through a higher marginal tax rate on that $70K. It is situation specific, but it has helped many clients not pay as much to the government.

The Straw Man of Estate Taxes

Remember, every asset you or your loved one die with is includable in your or their *gross estate*. Your gross estate includes items such as real estate, vehicles, IRAs, 401(k)s, checking and money market accounts, the value of all life insurance policies (unless in an irrevocable life insurance trust), investment accounts, art, precious metals, royalties, and more. Essentially, if you own it and it has value, then it is includable in the deceased's gross estate. The gross estate is just one measure or calculation of the estate of the deceased. Think of the total estate as the most substantial dollar amount, but it is just the starting point of calculations related to possibly incurring a federal estate tax liability.

The deceased would have to have an impressively large estate to be subject to *any* federal estate tax. Often, those wealthy individuals or families who do face potentially significant federal estate taxes have excellent estate planning done to prevent having to pay any federal estate taxes.

For our purposes, let's think of the gross estate as reflecting their entire asset total, minus any debts (liabilities) they owe on those assets. To be uncomplicated, from that large dollar amount (after subtracting their debts and liabilities), there are additional subtractions (deductions) as set out by IRS regulations, which I will pass over for our purposes of simplification and brevity. Following IRS guidelines, after all computations (subtractions), the *taxable estate* is the dollar amount that is subject to federal estate taxes. Even for wealthy people, the size of their gross estate is so much more substantial than the taxable estate because of all the subtractions or deductions, which help surviving family retain, if not all, a considerable portion of the estate of the deceased.

Please remember: either your attorney or your tax adviser will file with the IRS Form 706, sending it *no later than nine months* after the date of the decedent's death. IRS Form 706 is the federal estate tax form. Even though most deceased individuals in the US do not owe a cent of federal estate taxes, the IRS requires the filing of IRS Form 706 whether any tax payments are due or not.

In 2019, nearly $12 million was excludable from estate taxes. Just before I began my career, an individual with a taxable estate over $600,000 was subject to estate tax at rates of 55 percent to 60 percent versus 40 percent. You can see that the exclusion (or the excludable amount), that is, the amount not subject to estate taxes, has skyrocketed over the years. Each year, fewer taxpayers owe any estate taxes, and with the significant dollar amounts of the deceased's estate presently excludable, you can readily see why. Even better, if a wealthy couple set up what is known as AB trusts, which go by several other names, they can effectively double the amount of the exclusion from estate taxes. Double!

In 2019, a savvy couple with sound legal advice could come close to excluding nearly $24 million. In my estate planning classes, I get a laugh when I tease, "If your estate is larger than the current exclusion, please see me first after class." I also joke, "What a good problem this is to have!" Trust me, skilled attorneys working with knowledgeable tax, investment, and insurance professionals have a variety of practical solutions to fix that "problem."

Revocable Living Trusts

I serve more clients who do not have a revocable living trust than those who have a revocable living trust. However, particularly during the last ten years, I have seen an uptick in the usage of these type of trusts. Do you need one? A local attorney with more than forty years of experience indicated that in our state, the statutes are such that, in his opinion, almost no one needs a revocable living trust.

Then again, each state's estate-related statutes are different. Many clients have indicated that for them, according to their counsel, a revocable living trust is not a must-have. Instead, it is an option that offers salient benefits that they may prefer. There are some aspects of the revocable living trust that appeal to some individuals and their families. Only your legal adviser knows whether having a revocable living trust will serve you well or is not necessary for your situation.

I find when I teach my estate planning–related course that the only topic that seems to intimidate the class initially is the topic of trusts. I intend to demystify trusts so you will view them as approachable. A trust is a legal document that can be customized to fit exactly your needs within the limits of the statutes. There are a wide variety of trusts used for different purposes. By far, the revocable living trust is the most commonly used trust for estate planning purposes that I see.

If placing all trusts only into two hemispheres, in the first, there are trusts established while the person is alive, which is part of the title of a revocable *living* trust. The second hemisphere contains trusts that spring into existence when a person dies, and these are called testamentary trusts.

Suppose you own an asset in your name, single name, also called fee simple ownership, and you decide to move your asset (to retitle or rename who owns it) into a JTWROS account with your spouse or someone else. In contrast, let's look at single ownership of that identical asset that instead of choosing to retitle the ownership to a joint tenant with rights of survivorship account, you alternatively select to retitle your sole ownership name property into your revocable living trust.

You could choose to transfer from single name nearly anything, such as stocks, bonds, real estate, automobiles, checking, and money market accounts (and a whole lot more) into a revocable living trust in your name. Typically, the attorney has drawn up one revocable living trust for each spouse. (I have seen one revocable living trust drawn up for the couple, and that approach has worked well also; it tends to be attorney and client preference).

Let's look at the titling of mine as an example; I have the "Michael Wittenberg Revocable Living Trust, Dated XX, XX, 1992. Michael Wittenberg, Trustee." If you establish a revocable living trust, yours is likely to be titled similarly (based on the statutes of your state).

The person who chooses to place an asset into a trust is the grantor. So for simplicity, you own a single checking account and a separate money market account (MM). You are married, and you decide you no longer wish to keep your assets in single name. You could select to move your checking and MM into either joint name with your spouse (JTWROS) or to a revocable living trust.

Suppose your attorney advises you to set up a revocable living trust for you and a separate revocable living trust for your spouse. When you are placing or transferring an asset you own into a trust, the legal profession often calls you a grantor, but there are other equivalent terms such as a settlor or a trustor. I want to stay away from legalese so the concepts and broad outlines are approachable; I use language familiar to the layperson, not the precise language an attorney may use. While various names may be used as synonyms by nonattorneys, attorneys know when to use a given word that has a slightly different shade of meaning for their precision.

Please take out a sheet of white paper, or on your laptop, bring up a plain white unlined page. If you do this alongside my description rather than merely read this, your tactile involvement will likely help you understand it quicker and more deeply.

In the middle of the page, draw a square roughly two or three inches on each side (no precision required) and write the words *revocable living trust* in that square. On the left side of the page parallel to the square but closer to the left-hand margin, write the word *grantor*. Between the word *grantor* and the square, write the words *trust principal*. The owner, when they are placing their asset into the revocable living trust, is referred to as the grantor. The asset(s) that the grantor chooses to put in the trust is the trust principal. Above the box with *revocable living trust*, write the word *trustee(s)*. The trustee is the decision-maker regarding all trust assets. The trustee of a revocable living trust has the power of control.

Let's suppose your attorney drafted a trust that meets your specific needs, and in this case, the type of trust your attorney recommended as being most useful for you is a revocable living trust. In this example, you visit the financial institution that hosts your checking and money market (MM) accounts toting a copy of your new revocable living trust. You instruct the pleasant staffers that you want to change the ownership from your single name and have these two accounts instead be retitled (the property renamed) to your revocable living trust. Thus, your revocable living trust is now the titled (named) owner of both the checking and MM accounts that had been solely owned (titled and named) to you only.

Often, the staff will want to make a copy of only the first and last page of your trust document. Why? By copying the first page, they are sure that they have the proper titling (or ownership name) of your revocable living trust, as designed by your attorney. The title of your revocable living trust appears on your checking and money market (MM) *accounts* (however, it is salient to note, *not* necessarily on your *checks*).

By making a copy of the last page (or sometimes the last two pages) where both your signature and the notary's stamp and signature appears, the staff can see this document is duly signed and notarized. No one else needs to know that you have a revocable living trust (though it depends on the rules of the financial institution you use).

Although more checking and money market (MM) transactions are moving online, some individuals depend on their old-style checkbooks.

Ask the institution's staffer how your new checks will appear. Ask if instead of the titling of the trust (which you understand must be on the account reflecting the account's ownership) only your name and your address may appear on your checking and MM checkbooks rather than any trust information. Many institutions will permit that.

If your checking and money market accounts are solely in your name (as a single account), who could do anything they wanted with the assets in a sole-name ownership? You can. In the case of money market or checking, you can transfer those funds elsewhere. You can buy another asset with those funds, and you can spend all the funds in your accounts for needs or wants as you prefer. Also, you could decide to close the account. You control; you are the boss because you are the owner.

In your revocable living trust, who is usually the trustee? You are the trustee. It's your trust. What does being the trustee mean? You oversee the assets in the trust according to the terms of the trust that your attorney drew up customized to your needs and preferences, typically with impressive flexibility for you! Are you less powerful? No. You were the sole owner in a single-name account, and after the advice of your counsel, you may be the sole trustee of your revocable living trust.

You choose what assets you wanted to put into a single-name ownership or joint ownership or into a trust where the trust owns the asset. You are the trustee of that trust with complete control of the assets named or retitled to the trust. If you wanted to sell something you own in a single name, you sell it. You might sell an asset if the asset is in joint name, or you can sell the same asset if it was titled to or in the name of the trust. You can use trust assets to purchase other assets, just as you could use single- or joint-name assets to buy something you want. You can spend assets from your individual or single account, joint account, or revocable living trust account.

As trustee of your revocable living trust, you can remove any assets from the revocable living trust and retitle them to single- or joint-name ownership if you wish. That's a power you have as the trustee of your trust. Also, should you want to amend your trust because of a life change, your attorney can amend your trust with your signature. If you wish to end the trust entirely, you are the trustee, and you can empty all the assets and revoke your revocable living trust, keeping in mind the concept that being of sound mind is required to be able to sign legal documents.

What I find is off-putting to so many individuals, making trusts challenging to understand, is the nomenclature of trusts. Grantor, trustee, and trust principal sound to some as remote as if their assets are trapped forever, preventing their control, use, and enjoyment. If you share those apprehensions from old movie dramas of wealthy families fighting, set that aside when considering the most popular type of estate planning trust—the revocable living trust.

On certain types of trusts that your attorney may recommend and draw up for you, your attorney will get from the IRS a tax identification number, referred to as an estate identification number (EIN). As an example, an irrevocable life insurance trust (ILIT) requires an EIN. Unfortunately, this means separate tax filings each year for the ILIT, so more complexity and tax prep cost for you. The irrevocable life insurance trust, also called a wealth replacement trust (WRT), was much more prevalent when federal estate tax thresholds were much lower. I have seen no interest in ILITs or WRTs in several years as fewer and fewer US taxpayers are likely subject to pay any federal estate taxes.

In contrast, what is terrific about the revocable living trust is you use your social security number, just as you do on a single- or joint-ownership account. There's no separate tax filing. As you are accustomed to, IRS Form 1040 will do the trick, easy peasy.

If it's your trust, the entire time you maintain your revocable living trust while you are alive, who benefits from the trust? You do! Language is added to protect anyone else you love, such as your spouse or your adult children. Since you are not going to live forever, your attorney will include the names of all your remainder beneficiaries. You choose who your remainder beneficiaries are, just as you would list your heirs in your will, and you decide what assets to transfer to your revocable living trust. In jest, as you may hear on TV, "But wait, there's more."

How do attorneys afford individuals with a will and a revocable living trust a high degree of asset and inheritance privacy? Often, how I have seen the attorneys draw up the will when there is an accompanying revocable living trust, the will gives away no details except "to see the revocable living trust" for those details. If anyone read that person's will online, they'd know that there's a trust but know nothing else.

In the revocable living trust, usually about page 2, after the title page of the trust, there is a list of who gets what assets. Completely private. Only those who will receive assets as designated by the trust can read the trust, typically. I have seen very fancy printed revocable living trusts in beautiful binders that are quite thick. However, the distribution of assets page is as simple and clear as can be. The list often fits one page and indicates precisely who the recipients are and what is to be received by each of them.

Sometimes, I see a column of the names of asset recipients on the left-hand side of the page. In a second column on the right side of that page, there's either a list by the percentage or by dollar amount opposite the names of those recipients of the trustee's estate. Specific items may be listed to go to certain individuals.

Several times, I was made aware that the trustee of their own revocable living trust decided to change the dollar amounts or percentages of their bequests and even delete or add different heirs, both individuals and institutions. Instead of the need and expense of drafting an entirely new will, the trustee of their revocable living trust has their attorney change one page of their revocable living trust at minimal cost to the trustee. They asked their attorney if they need to update their will. If their will, in effect, said, "See the revocable living trust," their attorney may have advised them they do not need a new will. They merely may need to change one page of their revocable living trust indicating who gets what. Once again, easy peasy.

In the case of arguments leading to years of family estrangement, I have seen a significant recipient deleted entirely from the distribution of assets page, and after the rift ended, that same excluded individual once again was named as a trust remainder beneficiary. I have been asked, "If I die before my sib, will my sibling ever find out that I was so furious and hurt I removed them as a recipient under my revocable living trust, only to later reinstate them?" The answer is no. When you die, whatever you have decided regarding your current distribution of assets as indicated on your list is all the revocable living trust remainder beneficiaries see.

If you are partnered but not legally married, please seek advice from your attorney ASAP. You or your partner may have wills that leave all your assets to one another, for example. However, if a family member contests your will or, even worse, if you don't have a valid will at death, whatever intentions or wishes you may have to leave assets to your partner may not occur; your will potentially could be set aside as a result of a will contest. If you have no will, your state of domicile has an elaborate scheme of how assets are conveyed to next of kin, not to your partner. However, your attorney may recommend a revocable living trust, in addition to a will, if you are in a situation where a will contest is likely. Let's say a close family member disapproves of your relationship with your partner; your revocable living trust may enable your partner to receive everything you intend.

How Influential Are You?

In almost all family situations where I was made aware of inheritance decisions, all adult children of a given family typically are treated equally regarding the distribution of assets at the death of their last parent. Often, this is using a parent's will or the revocable living trust (and using beneficiary clauses and designations as well as PODs and TODs where appropriate).

However, I now see the following situation with increasing frequency. It is not uncommon that the aging or ill parent(s) moves to live near or with one of their adult children. A common experience for the adult child who is caring for their parent(s) is that their sibs may not be able to participate in caregiving or may choose not to do so. Sometimes, the caregiver's siblings may want to provide meaningful assistance. However, one or more of the sibs may live so far away that assisting is impractical, if not impossible.

I can happily report I have seen circumstances where everyone is pitching in without strife among them for the benefit of their loved one. However, repeatedly, even in a family that has many adult children, I see one adult child carrying more than 90 percent of the caregiving responsibility for aging, ill parents. The adult child living nearby their parent often takes on most of the caregiving. The caregiver may have already retired, while their younger sibs still have jobs. And knowing that their parent's time is short, they want to be with their parent to provide excellent care up to the last moment in a labor of love.

More often, I have heard, "Michael, I am not going to let Mom go without my help, and no one else in my family can or is choosing to help. I feel stuck. Please don't think that I do not love or do not want to help my mom. It's not that at all. I just wish I had some help from my brothers and sisters. No matter what happens, I am going to take good care of my mom like she took good care of me." This situation I have seen repeated many times.

As a result, I have worked with clients who wanted to leave more of their assets to the adult child who did so much for them at this time of their greatest need. One individual told me while expressing anger and disgust that one of his adult children living in town had "not lifted one finger" to help him as he aged while another of his adult children had been magnificent in their caregiving. He wanted 100 percent of his estate to go to the attentive caregiver and leave nothing for anyone else.

Naturally, I recommended he visit his attorney, pronto. If the attorney was not averse to the idea, I also suggested he consider talking with anyone who would expect to be an heir and explain his decision face-to-face so they would have an opportunity to respond. From our discussion, the feared emotional reaction left Dad unwilling to broach this topic. I have found family discussions help lead to acceptance over time, even when the initial response is volatile.

Picture this simple vignette: the surviving parent chooses to leave her entire estate to one of two children. This father says nothing to the adult child he decides not to make an heir so that at his death, when learning they had been disinherited, the individual feels hurt, and livid. Feeling wronged, the disinherited son seeks an attorney. Let's even suppose that the son received a minor amount of money. Even though not technically accurate, the son was effectively disinherited. "I leave my son, Henry, one dollar [$1] for his lack of caregiving."

Is a legal battle prevented? The son's counsel may argue that the adult child who received the entire estate was with Dad so much that she had "undue influence" over Dad, and that is why this unjust division of assets occurred. How does the daughter prove the negative? What I find ironic is that the excellent care provided by one adult child for a parent may be the club used against them by a sibling who didn't help their parent, and though they may have no right to any of their father's assets, they want half.

I believe a knowledgeable attorney can help a family in many ways, especially with thorny situations like these. Please do not focus only on cost; give equal weight to what benefits you will receive.

Suppose you are a parent who wants to give an uneven distribution of assets to heirs who might expect an equal distribution of assets. If the heirs are your adult children, typically, there's no requirement for you to split your estate equally among your children, though it is what I often see occur. They are your assets to distribute at your death as you wish. True (though there are exceptions).

You have two broad choices. You can sow the seeds, enabling family members to become closer after your death, through your wise preparation. Alternatively, you can metaphorically set off a bomb amid all your children by your choices, your silence, and by you not using skilled legal advice to make your division of assets less likely to lead to WWIII after your death.

There are various steps counsel can take for your benefit, so your unequal division of assets is as buttoned up as much as possible so that anyone unhappy realizes there is a high bar for them to cross over to prevail via litigation.

When a parent is still living, there is an opportunity for dialogue. I have found this to be crucial and positive for families. A family meeting is sometimes held at the holidays; a family visit gives both the parent and their children a chance to discuss the parent's wishes and plans. If any heir is unhappy, they can lobby for what they think is fair. At least that adult child had an opportunity to make their viewpoint known.

This lobbying or rebuttal may or may not sway the parent to rethink their asset distribution plans. At a minimum, the parent has explained their logic why they want to distribute *their* assets unequally, so the family hears it in person from the source; the heir getting less (or nothing) then has an immediate opportunity to respond to the parent. Ideally, this explanation by the parent occurs long before the parent's death, though sometimes that's not possible. It may be a deathbed family meeting, making the emotional volatility of the meeting potentially much worse.

With the parent's estate distribution disclosure, at least everything is out in the open, allowing both generations to hear and adjust to each other's comments. When I say disclosure, I do not mean specificity. I have seen many loving parents not wanting to tell their children their net worth for a variety of reasons, including they didn't want to be asked for money and feel compelled to loan money they may later need.

Still, at the family meeting, they may say something like, "We wanted to explain to you our views on inheritance. As you know, we are charitably minded, so 25 percent of our estate will go to the charities we strongly support, and each of the three of you will receive 25 percent apiece. We did not want you surprised by this after our deaths. While this is our choice, as these are our assets, we love you, so we wanted to inform you of our current estate plans and hear your thoughts on what we have decided."

I have listened to parents tell me, "Since we want each of our adult children to know that we loved them as much as our other adult children, our estate is to be divided equally among them." However, I have had parents wrestle with this situation: "Our oldest child owns a thriving business, but our other two are not financially successful. The oldest doesn't need anything, and we know the other two truly need our assets when the second one of us dies."

My first observation is that the adult child who owns a successful business when you established your estate plan may be contending with a failing business when the estate plan activates due to death, let us suppose, seven years later.

My second observation is that some adult children perceive that if they get less than a sibling, they were loved or liked less by their parents than were any of their sibs who received more than they did. Even when they logically know that this is not true, emotionally, for some adult children, there's a sting to this. So I have overwhelmingly found it better if parents explain, particularly to the adult child or children, who will receive less and disclose this to them in a discussion. Discovering this with no warning after the death of the second of the two parents can emotionally devastate the child or children who receive less, compounded because that was unexpected.

If you want your adult children to remember you, surprise them with an unannounced inherited amount that is less than their sibs, and I assure you that child will never forget you; however, probably not the way you'd prefer. Consider talking with them.

The Probate and Estate Settlement Processes Are
so Much Fun (Not!); Let's Do Extra Work!

In addition to privacy, a powerful advantage that motivates many clients' attorneys to set up a revocable living trust for them is to avoid a process known as ancillary probate. Suppose you or your only living parent own a modest mountain cabin or a beautiful lake or beach house in another state. After death, the executor or administrator (or generically the "personal representative") works to settle the estate in the county that was the official domicile of the deceased (where they voted, paid local taxes, and had their mail sent, among other requirements). However, typically, if a property was owned by the deceased in another state, a new probate process must be completed. Oh, joy! Usually, that other or ancillary probate process occurs in the county (typically at the courthouse) of property's location (the beach house, for example).

I have listened to clients who served as executors of a loved one's estate understandably grouse about the cost, inconvenience, delay, and most especially the time that it takes to close out the ancillary probate process. While this may seem minor, suppose you are serving as an executor and you are employed; here's what can happen. I have learned about clients who preferred to handle as much of this as they could themselves, taking a day off from work, traveling six hours away to another state, believing they had brought with them all the documents they needed, only to learn something was missing. Wash, rinse, repeat. How easy is it for an executor or personal representative to meet an essential duty they have—to protect the property—when they live six or more hours away?

If ancillary probate is required, your in-state attorney can contact a law office in the other state to have this second attorney handle as much of this process as possible. Yes, this entails additional fees and legal costs. Your attorney may even list the charges of ancillary probate on their invoices to you for your convenience.

Another compelling reason to establish a revocable living trust is to dispense with the cost and irritation of ancillary probate. Some attorneys set up a revocable living trust for their clients so they can retitle all the properties the client owns in states other than their state of domicile. Typically, having all properties retitled obviates the need for ancillary probate. Thus, all those out-of-state properties along with all the probate assets in the deceased's home state conveniently avoid dealing with some county courthouse in another state. If you or your spouse or parents have a property in another state, talk with your attorney about what they recommend is the best way to handle the situation.

While on the topic of real estate, this is crucial to be aware of: typically homeowner's property insurance is priced under the presumption that the homeowner occupies the residence. If one of your parents is deceased, for example, and you move your other parent to a retirement home to receive a level of care for them referred to as assisted living, your parent's house may now be an unoccupied dwelling. Some insurance companies have a thirty-day window in their policies, after which they charge a higher premium if a residence is vacant.

The insurance company expects that the insured report that the dwelling is unoccupied. As is intuitive, if someone is home, all kinds of issues that could lead to a property casualty claim are prevented or caught early by the occupants. I canvass my classes comprised of middle-aged to older adult students to see if anyone is aware of this issue, and invariably, several students in each class are aware of it. I poll those students to ascertain the magnitude of the premium increase that insurance company charged when a family member's home became unoccupied. I have heard a wide range of premium price increases from their self-reports, which I cannot verify. The percentages students indicated ran from +20 percent to as high as the premium tripling.

Some students have acknowledged that they haven't reported that their parent's residence is now unoccupied to their property casualty agents to keep the premium the same amount. When filing a claim, it's easy for the claims adjuster to figure out no one has been living at the dwelling for months and deny the claim. I think it is worth the extra premium cost to protect the property. If you are in the situation where you happen to be the executor, that role must preserve the property.

Lions, Tigers, and Siblings, Oh My!

The iron law for some adult siblings is that the volume of their noisy fault finding is in inverse proportion to their effort supporting the person in need or their caregiver. In the worst examples, one or more siblings complain and harangue incessantly but never lift a finger to help.

Fortuitously, I have met many outstanding individuals and families, including siblings and nonfamily caregivers. If that were the only reality, this book would be a lot shorter. If you are an adult sibling on the receiving end of sniping and criticism, I will guide you through what you may do to be less impacted by their static that will not get you incarcerated. Setting boundaries with loved ones may be difficult, yet it is so crucial. We'll look at what you can do and what you cannot do.

You only control your thoughts, feelings, and behaviors. Once you choose to believe and act on that immutable truth, your life changes for the better, much better. You may want an adult sibling, a spouse, an adult child—someone, anyone—to do something useful, to step up and help you share the work in providing care for Mom and Dad or whomever. However, you can embrace or reject acceptance that you can only control what you do. Though you control your behavior, even there, you don't control the outcome of your action no matter how well intended. You only own your input; you don't control the output despite how hard you try. Sad but true.

In Western philosophy, we tend to think that if we made the right decision, we get a favorable outcome. Other philosophical strands delink decisions and outcomes positing that all anyone can do is to make the wisest decision they can at that moment after careful deliberation. Thus, the result delivered is not solely controlled by the quality of the decision but rather by many following incidents that were unknowable at the time of the decision. To me, this latter view seems more like how life works.

Lack of support can seem and may be so unfair! You can feel like you're drowning from the situation, and inwardly, you'd like to scream at your adult siblings, "How about throw me a life preserver every blue moon. I'm doing everything while all you're doing is whining. If you don't help me, at least stop dropping a boatload of anchors on me."

You can make yourself sick with anger and frustration if you expect that your sibs should help you. "Don't you mean, Michael, that their selfish unhelpfulness is what's making me feel furious?" No. Though I readily see how you may think that's the cause, "But if my brother and sister would only help me take care of Mom and Dad, then I wouldn't feel so livid! I am exhausted, and I get no support when I need their help." I agree it certainly appears that way. I understand why you feel depleted. I have immense respect and compassion for caregivers as I have served in that role and understand some of its many challenges.

I have seen the caregiving sib or spouse be overwhelmed with the myriad needs of Mom's or Dad's illness or their recent death and its aftermath, and they feel alone. They also may feel inadequate to complete the multitude of unfamiliar required tasks. Additionally, you may feel guilty over not being able to do all you wish to do for your loved ones and possibly feel a second dollop of guilt over not being able to be as effective with a spouse, children, at work, or with the rest of your daily life.

I have seen the caregiver get so sick, even dying, before their ill spouse or parent, worn out while overextended among home, work, children, and taking care of their loved one, without meaningful respite. Caregiving can be significant pressure on a marriage or one's career. You may realize all this far too well. Sometimes, where you can manage the tasks, you feel hurt because you feel abandoned or you feel angry since you judge the situation as your sibs don't care enough about Mom or Dad or about you and what sacrifices you've chosen to make for the well-being of your parents. "Tag, you're it" isn't fun and doesn't feel fair at all. You may feel disrespected, taken for granted, and used.

"Michael, I am doing so much for Mom or Dad or both." Agreed! That's not in doubt. "Well, I cannot convince my sibs of that." True! You are correct; you cannot control the thoughts, opinions, and beliefs of anyone else. Please be kind and gentle with yourself; please stop self-administering daily doses of anger, resentment, and bitterness while fracturing your family bonds.

Whomever your situational "opponent" is, they have no time to focus on considering changing their attitudes from an unhelpful critic to supporting you if they are spending their time, emotional response, and energy being adversarial on the second war front, which they think you started. They focus on proving themselves correct. They will unswervingly "guard the battlements" protecting their egos while justifying their views. It may be just a series of rationalizations, but those can be intractable and fiercely defended. This war leaves you in the same undesirable situation. As you lower your expectations, you stop ruminating negatively or fighting a draining unwinnable battle, on what you are powerless.

Here's where you may disagree, however, please entertain these thoughts. Though it doesn't seem correct, you unintentionally made yourself angry by reacting to the nonsupport of your sibs. They will do or not do whatever they prefer.

You may believe you know everything you think there is to know about your sibs' current situations, but your sibs may face significant problems that they may feel embarrassed to share that precludes aiding you in your role as caregiver or if you need care.

Have you ever thought negatively about the behavior of someone else only to change your opinion 180 degrees when you learned of their unannounced plight? Yes, you must observe and discern as part of successful living; however, do you judge far more often than needed? I think most of us do. Do you like to be judged? I haven't yet met anyone who does. You can put anyone "into the dock" as you wish, without an ounce of a positive result for all your self-induced turmoil. You are not a bounty hunter, jailer, or executioner (shucks); you are a sibling.

Alternatively, you can also choose to view it as, "If I didn't have any siblings or a spouse or adult children to help me, I would not be creating and storing judgmental ill will that doesn't hurt them. It hurts me." Someday, all the chores will be finished. Will your contact with your siblings also be finished? Is that the outcome you seek?

I am sorry for any pain you may be going through. In this chapter, I attempted to focus your attention to common unwanted, unpleasant feelings that can beset caregivers, which many people have shared with me over many years. I am not trying to induce clinical depression. I am underscoring how demanding it can be as a caregiver, which many loving caregivers know all too well. So why restate the obvious? Consider some of the emotions you may be feeling; to prevent burnout, your self-care is essential. To this, I hear this response: "Michael, the self-care I know I need is precluded by all I have to do for my spouse or mom and dad." Understood. All I ask you to consider is to try not to minimize the importance of respite for yourself if you are the caregiver. Your needs are legitimate. Please ask those you love for what you need.

You and I realize how difficult it can be to work in the department of easier said than done to let your expectations go. The more you lower your expectations, the happier you will be. If you are finding this impossible to do, seek professional counseling to help you express and release your feelings surrounding the demanding responsibilities you have chosen to undertake for someone you love.

Are You Acting Like Your Siblings' Parent?

When you return home at the holidays, are you revisiting old behavior patterns as if you and your siblings have traveled back to your childhood or adolescence? If you think that your sibs are not spending enough time with the person you are concerned about, avoid saying or writing imperious phrases like, "You need to visit Mom." You may consider this phrasing innocuous. It's not. You may sound to your siblings as if you are acting in a self-appointed supervisory role. Your sisters and brothers may bristle at your comments and purposely do the opposite to thwart your directive spitefully. "But, Michael, all I said to my sister is that she needs to [should, ought to, must] visit Mom, and we got into a big fight [unsurprisingly]."

Alternatively, "Michael, my sister lives just an hour from my dad, and she only visits once per quarter, if that much. My father occasionally tells me he'd like to see her. He asks why she rarely visits him and says that sometimes he feels so lonely. I feel terrible, and I am so furious at my sister she doesn't care about Dad." (Emotional, self-poisoning judgment—potentially your sister may not care that you are angry with her; she may even relish it.)

People do what they do because it seems to make sense to them, and they believe it serves them well even when it is self-injurious. Your values, though raised together, are not their values. You cannot impose your values on anyone else (we are revisiting what you do not control). You may find that with time, some sibs or other family begin to buy in. You may be correct that they will never lift a finger to help you. However, when you look back throughout the illness, sibs' behaviors sometimes change for the better, even when it seems most unlikely. In any case, you do not control either outcome. Difficult to accept, difficult to do, but necessary for your well-being.

First, do you have to be the messenger? Don't knee-jerk an affirmative answer. Is there another route that will enable the passage of the message without raising a ruckus with your family, leaving you feeling like an unwilling bouncer? Also remember, sometimes, sibling rifts can be so fraught due to prior history that parental illness may further compound the tension and disagreement. You are not required to be the messenger. "Dad, I don't want to get in a battle with Susan. If I pass on what you are kindly sharing with me, it may get ugly, which could be counterproductive for our family. Would you prefer to tell Susan about your loneliness and your wish for Susan to visit more and the reasons she does not? I prefer not to be in the messenger role." Put the ball back in Dad's court. He is a grown-up, and he may decline to say a word to Susan, but you didn't get vacuumed into acting in a manner that may worsen a delicate situation with your sib.

If Susan went on the offensive, "And what did you say to Dad when he said those things about me?" If correct, you can say, "I just listened to what Dad had to say. I thought it best not to comment. I do not want to be in a 'no win' position between you and Dad, Susan."

If it is appropriate for you to assist with the transmission of messages, how can you send a positive message about what pains your dad and you so much emotionally? You can give your sister a call or write an email, sticking solely to the facts while considering tone. Attempting to soften your written or spoken delivery, often an angry or sarcastic tone, is a much more powerful incendiary device than the words themselves.

"Susan, Dad has indicated that he feels lonely [fact, which you heard and set down unfiltered in the role of scribe]. He said, 'I don't know why Susan doesn't visit more often,' and he also said that he 'wished Susan would visit more.'" Notice what the last two phrases lack: the word *you*. Read the next sentence carefully. You could say, "Dad asked me why you don't visit more often" versus, as above,

"Dad said to me, 'I don't know why Susan doesn't visit more often.'" Recounting what your father said takes the speaker or writer out of the equation, yet it sends a powerful emotional message to Susan, who will choose what, if anything, to do with it. You are merely a neutral messenger and then an observer.

If you wish to create a fight in no time, start a sentence with *you* followed by a negative, and it will be game on! "You didn't take out the trash." "You didn't pick up your clothes." "You left the lights on." "You were late picking me up." Those statements may be factual. You are well familiar with the scientific law that for every action, there's an equal and opposite reaction.

If you intend on proving the accuracy of that seminal scientific observation, all you need to do is make what sounds like an accusation, which you may view as a simple declarative statement. In response to your word choice, the hearer may feel defensive and put up high emotional walls to protect themselves. *You* nearly ensures that understanding your viewpoint will come in a distant second to their need for a passionate defense.

Return to the most fundamental question: What's your aim? What positives are you trying to achieve? You seek communication and maybe some follow-up prosocial behavior. What was the equal and opposite reaction? You may instead receive rationalizations and even encounter verbal aggressiveness from the listener.

A favorite tool of the listener who thinks they are under attack is to adroitly change the topic entirely to, "But you didn't do X" to deflect your concerns, hoping you will take their bait with you feeling compelled, purposely triggered, to defend against their issue. Their issue may be nothing more than a false equivalence; even if legit, don't take the bait. Tit-for-tat arguing over supposed equivalent dueling "court cases" doesn't achieve much for anyone. Is your aim to assert that you are correct? Alternatively, do you want to be heard empathetically? What's more important, being right or maintaining a relationship?

"Good Fences Make Good Neighbors"

If you receive a countervailing argument, as previously mentioned, it is critical that you call time-out and set your boundary, which in this case is the method of operation you want followed to fight fair. "I will discuss your issue, however, only after we finish discussing the topic that I introduced first." If they don't agree, consider ending the discussion to create a time-out for a cooldown. "I feel upset now. I would like to think and not discuss anything further at this time because I want to show my respect to you, not escalate anger, and consider what you just said." If you feel you'll melt under a potentially withering response, write out some polite phrases to help you control your behavior. I get that this may be so difficult for anyone to do now. However, it works.

You have indicated what you wish. You have considered a boundary, which is a rule that works for you and which you are stating is that which you seek honored. You control that you explained what you prefer as a mode of operation to either avoid a verbal fight or to respectfully fight if you do. Can you control the response of your sibling or spouse? No. However, you can choose not to play their game; you can avoid taking their bait. You control taking some time out for yourself.

You can exit the room to de-escalate the conflict. Doing so allows you to collect your thoughts, and it is a powerful technique to elevate your position. Exiting with an explanation as to the reason for doing so, offered with kind words and tone, is a tool to help define and defend your boundary. Using the word *you* is unlikely to garner what you seek, such as understanding of your viewpoint, empathy over how you feel, and willing buy-in for a recommitment to the desired behavior you seek.

"Don't Take the Bait"

So you agree only you control your behavior, but that hasn't changed the tone or actions of your sibs one bit. What may help you a lot with your sibs is to consider the phrase, "Don't take the bait." Your sibs, spouse, children, friends, and coworkers know how to hook you. They are experts at getting a rise out of you. They may not realize what they are doing, or they may be baiting the hook for you on purpose and with enthusiasm. Please repeat after me: "I will not take their bait." Though initially confusing, like any skill, you'll get better at adroitly avoiding the hook over time with practice. Eventually, you will see the snare up ahead and dodge it.

Using a different metaphor, they will keep pushing your buttons; you hardly can stop that behavior, though I'll discuss some techniques that may assist you in making the button harder for your sibs, spouse, or others to reach. However, you can choose to disconnect the button they are pushing by not reacting as they are hoping and as they expect.

"Michael, my brother calls me and grills me on why I didn't do this and that, and I feel so upset. He always has the right answer, conveniently for him, only after the fact. However, he doesn't do anything to help me. He complains." Your siblings cannot stop what you view as your message, which they may view as static. You may feel angry and discounted by their consistent message to you, which you hear as their noise. Though you want it to stop, which you can request of them, you are unlikely to be able to enforce your request. We teach people how to treat us.

First Things First

Where may your action steps with sibs or other family members beneficially begin? Canvas your siblings what their thoughts are on the present or emerging situation. Whatever they tell you, write a brief paragraph or two of a restatement. Send it first to the sib who shared their views with you after amending what your brother or sister may have reflected with you regarding the content of your initial restatement. Send them the revised version to approve. Then ask that sib if they permit their ideas and concerns to be shared. If they green-light sending it to your siblings or other family members, see what feedback you get from everyone else potentially involved.

Sometimes, you will receive wildly different responses. Sometimes, a sib or other invited family member or friend will not respond. You can send an email explaining and initially letting off the hook those who did not respond with something like, "I value and appreciate hearing from everyone. All your ideas, comments, and feelings are welcome, and I will consider them respectfully. To solicit everyone's input while making progress, I am requesting all responses by date X. Though I am undertaking this organizing process, one concern I have is who will lead the process of determining what needs doing for Mom beyond this initial effort."

Categorize the responses you receive into feelings, facts, opinions, suggestions. Again, get buy-in from as many family members involved in allowing you to do a brief restatement of the responses by category. You will decide whether you are better served to indicate the name of who wrote or said what or whether family dynamics promote listing all the responses without attribution. Your goal is to invite everyone who wants their voice to be heard to be and feel heard. Whether you or another family member accept the task of reading the pulse of the family on the crisis (such as severe illness or death), canvassing for inclusion may help unify relationships even if it is challenging to develop a unified plan of action.

Then ask, "Who is volunteering to do what?" If because of geographic distance or other factors a given relative cannot physically help, what compensatory activities will they undertake as their contribution? "Since you get four weeks of vacation per year, will you use one of those weeks to spend with Dad so my immediate family and I can have a week's respite taking a vacation?"

If you are already amid extensive caregiving, you may also have to push on to this second organizational task. You may think you have no time to do this, but this will save you time. Write down precisely what you think Mom, Dad, or whoever is ill needs to have done. Alternatively, if working on estate settlement chores, write down all tasks. Be concrete. List as many of the actions or activities your loved one needs or the functions of estate settlement that are outstanding. Also, list the time that you are spending each week on all the helper tasks you are doing. Get the facts; track how you are spending your time as a caregiver.

Third, and this is where your power may lie, create a column for the cost of your time. If you are employed, you may have two columns, one for the income you lost being out of work to serve as a caregiver and a second column for the going rate in your locale for the work you did helping Mom or Dad. The going rate for support personnel may be twenty to thirty dollars per hour, but you may lose forty dollars per hour in pay when out of work.

Most caregivers tell me their role is stressful enough without having a carping sibling faultfinding always. Attaching a dollar amount to needed tasks, as if employing someone to help your loved one, multiplied by the many hours you spend assisting can get siblings' attention quickly.

"Taking Dad to the doctor" may not remotely explain the scope of the work you are choosing to do as you help your dad. What are its components? How long does it take? Write down each chore and how long each task typically takes, and list it in a time range. "It usually takes me three hours to take Dad to the doctor. However, some of our trips have taken as much as five hours. Here's the monthly total of hours for April that I spent on taking Dad to the doctor." If you prefer, write down the tasks on a calendar. Here's what actions I took on Mom's behalf last month, day by day, with the time listed when the activity started and concluded.

"Dad usually needs to see his various health-care providers seven times per month, though some months he has had as many as thirteen health provider appointments. Here is what I do before we leave for the doctor to get Dad ready to leave, and then here's what I do for Dad once we return home." If your sibs never do the activity, then they may have no clue what's involved.

You benefit yourself, as well, when you see a comprehensive list of what you are doing for your loved one and the considerable time it takes. This list helps to establish a clear picture and a baseline for everyone you share this information to attempt to help your siblings and other family members understand the scope of the needs and tasks for the person who needs care.

Consider the first column, where you are listing your support activities, as you are qualifying your efforts to attempt to create more accurate perceptions of what is involved. The time and expense or cost columns allow you to quantify your work as a caregiver. This comprehensive picture of the myriad chores sometimes jolts the complaining siblings into silence, especially if you ask this: "Since you are out of state or since you are choosing not to take on these tasks [no snark, just the facts, ma'am], how much of Mom's cost of care will you help defray?" You may hear crickets or get an earful; however, you can now metaphorically build a wall marking acceptable behavior you expect to see, or, said differently, you set a boundary to clearly define what you consider and require to be in-bounds and out-of-bounds behavior. You don't control your siblings' response;

however, you have politely notified them of what is acceptable to you. How may you behave to maintain the solidity of the boundaries you set?

If you don't expect to see a dime of support and no meaningful assistance with caregiving, you may say in a pleasant tone or write something like, "As your choice is to provide neither care nor help with the cost of care, I prefer your unsolicited direction and criticism end" (notice no use of the word "you.") If you continue to receive their loud static, whatever polite, clear, firm message you choose to send, you may benefit from repeating it verbatim. In effect, your message is, though I do *not* recommend you write it this way, "If you don't want to put skin in the game, you do not get to tell me what to do, and you don't get to criticize me. However, you are permitted to be grateful" (notice way too much use of the word "you," which will boomerang back to writer or speaker).

Useful Psychobabble, Accent on the Word *Useful*

Here's an example where the patient was entirely correct and the professional failed. Once, a surgeon shared a story with me from years earlier that he so regretted, which he characterized as the worst remark he had ever said to a patient in over three decades of practice. As I remember his story, exhausted from several surgeries that day, he met with a prospective surgical patient who was struggling with acceptance of the potential for disfigurement caused by disease. She was not realistic and cooperative from the surgeon's vantage point; however, he was not potentially going to have a part of his body sliced off.

He indicated with remorse that he told the patient, "I didn't give you cancer." That cold, unprofessional remark, unsurprisingly, abruptly ended the consult as the livid patient left on her way to find herself another surgeon. I could see it etched in the surgeon's face how much that one sentence haunted him.

We can all readily access great compassion for the patient over that cruel and needless rebuke. It's much harder for us to have empathy for the surgeon, though I was impressed that the surgeon didn't shrink from accurately appraising his failed verbal behavior. His pain was evident years later.

I am not urging you to accept unprofessional behavior from anyone. As an example, sometimes, a security "tender offer" may be sent to my clients with the scary-sounding equivalent of "You must act immediately, or all life on earth will cease solely because of your inaction. Last time you were slow to act, you caused the dinosaurs to become extinct." The language of securities attorneys is such that the offer is impenetrable to the reader, and both its supposed import and required immediacy may hook highly intelligent clients into feeling anxious or fearful. It is so easy for the client to misunderstand securities lit, jumping to a false confusion. Plus, it is an intrusion in their already harried day.

Clients are human, so they get angry. Their anger, fear, and anxiety may be free-floating. It is probably not solely directed at the company creating the chore and uncertainty by sending the offer, not at themselves for being overwrought over nothing, and not at me because the proposal is in my domain. Maybe some of it is directed at all the above.

Ask yourself this, and be observant: what occurred within you when you paid attention to the underlying cause of your last bout of anger? In asking yourself this question, focus deeper than the symptom level. If it's not clear enough, try this. The next time you feel angry, consider the following: Did you feel anxious? Did you feel disrespected? Both?

Thoughts and feelings of anxiousness or losing face, having our self-concept assaulted, and appearing to be treated dismissively can lead to anger unless we realize what's happening and short-circuit those unpleasant thoughts and feelings.

You are traveling on an interstate highway. A young male in another vehicle, driving at a high rate of speed, maneuvers dangerously. You are compelled to take evasive action to avoid an accident. You did nothing to precipitate this unexpected risk; however, for your safety, you needed to respond immediately adroitly. You skillfully succeed. You are safe, and so are your passengers.

An individual can generate feelings of road rage. Have you ever thought, *My loved ones and I were nearly in a wreck. I could have totaled my auto*? These thoughts couple with the feelings of anxiousness and fear of how close you came to a disaster that you did not create as you were driving responsibly. You may also think and feel disrespected that someone dangerously driving showed no respect for you and no concern for your safety. "He is selfish. His life counts, while life counts for nothing to him. I want revenge."

In the vignette, the danger you experienced was real. Your feelings of fear were not real, but yes, while flooded with hormones, they felt as real as the danger. You sense a loss of face. You may feel enraged. It seems to happen instantaneously and seems nearly uncontrollable.

Though scary, anxiety and fear may have left you upset with deep anger. Sagaciously, you choose not to react aggressively to prevent further escalating the situation since you have deftly avoided a crash. You may fantasize committing some act of painful retribution, but you have or quickly regained control over your behavior. Soundly, you do not behave rashly or act illegally to avoid potentially severe negative consequences.

Has such a scenario happened to you? Unfortunately, it is all too common. Most people avoid overreacting, but despite their admirable self-control, it remains for them an unpleasant and frightening event. Those who surrender their control and go on the attack end up as the lead story of the local news.

If that were to happen to you in the future, how could you prevent the anxiety, fear, loss of face, and anger from being triggered? Do you control the thoughts upon which you act? If you view ideas as a mental activity that wafts into your conscious awareness like clouds that you watch sailing in and out of your mind, you could produce a completely different set of thoughts and emotions. "Oh, Michael, that's not possible. Every driver would react as you described above."

The mental technique some counselors use themselves and teach their clients is to substitute a much more benign vignette immediately that doesn't drag violent thoughts and unpleasant feelings with it. Reframe the scenario above. What if you now visualize that young man entirely differently. Suppose you realized that he is about to be a dad for the first time. He was racing to the hospital when he learned his wife had gone into labor. He did not intend to cause you risk of injury or loss of face; in fact, he didn't realize his poor driving impacted you. It was not about you at all, though the repercussions for you had you not successfully responded could have been injurious.

However, you are unhurt, though you may feel upset and emotionally drained as organic chemicals released to protect you in emergencies washed through you. Have you never made a driving mistake that made another driver feel similarly to how you felt?

Try this technique. I have used it successfully on the highway, and it is a useful tool to short-circuit all the unpleasant emotions that come with drivers who make errors. It may take you some practice; however, you can master it. I do not include this to assist you when facing unpleasant driving situations; it is added to show how you can reframe what you think from what's uncomfortable and burdensome to something far more benign. We don't control the behavior of another driver; we do control our reactions, thoughts, and feelings.

It is impossible to stress enough how our expectations can trap and harm us. When I was younger, I used to think I would be happy only if or when some events occurred. As soon as I get that job, marry, buy a home, become a father, receive a promotion, or reach a financial goal, I would become happier. Do you push happiness forward, waiting for its arrival when you achieve some accomplishment or future circumstance? "When I . . ." doesn't work. Any joy, no matter how great, over actual developments tends to be fleeting because those occurrences or events are external to us. Feelings of happiness and self-worth are thought to be "inside jobs." You feel happy not due to the attainment of extrinsic goals, as satisfying as they may be, but instead, you choose to be actively grateful, and *your feelings of gratitude lead you to feel happy.*

When much younger, I thought I would feel more grateful as my life circumstances improved as those would produce greater happiness. That's backward. If you practice focusing on being thankful for everything, big and small, your level of satisfaction increases immensely. Gratitude isn't an outgrowth of joy. Gratitude is a precondition or precursor to the development and growth of feelings of happiness. The more you appreciate everything, the happier you will become. It then becomes about how you look at the world, your attitude and viewpoint. "Most people are as happy as they make up their minds to be" goes the wisdom of Mark Twain. It's true.

Lottery winners who receive tens of millions of dollars return to their typically happiness thermostat setting about six months after they win.

I could become irritated when other people failed to deliver. I expected X, or the response I wanted to receive is X, or I did X for them. Why isn't that being reciprocated? I came to realize that my disappointment was much less about their failure to behave in a manner I preferred and much more about my expectations of their behavior. As my expectations plummeted, my happiness soared.

Communicate Your Preferences to Your Loved Ones

Though only age seventy-two at the time, my mom's gradually worsening emphysema COPD, unfortunately, impacted her terribly until she died at age seventy-four. My mother said, "Michael, thankfully, you do not understand what it feels like when you cannot draw a breath." It must be an indescribably horrible panicky feeling.

Nearly the entire last year of my mother's life was excruciating for her. She would remind me occasionally, sometimes in a joking way, that I, her oldest son and health-care POA (HPOA or MPOA), who lived just a few miles from her, had to be sure to do two things for her. First, I was to do nothing to prolong her life. Second, I was to do everything I could to be sure she felt as little discomfort as possible.

Starting about ten months before she died, my mom was in and out of the hospital. Fortunately, a savvy nurse had a gentle, realistic discussion with my mother while I happened to be visiting. The nurse inquired if my mother want to talk with someone from hospice. My mother agreed, and a representative from the hospice visited her in her hospital room. Thus began her contact with the excellent staff and volunteers at the hospice. She and I could have never praised the team at our local hospice enough.

Throughout, my mother kept reminding me of her wishes. She'd joke, "If you keep me alive for one extra minute, I will come back to haunt you." We'd both laugh. I attempted to reassure her I would do my utmost to follow her wishes. Her repetition of her wants proved to be but one of the many gifts she gave me during my life.

Once again, my mother returned to the hospital less than two weeks before her death. It was in the evening, and I was the only visitor in her room while my mother seemed to be sleeping. Suddenly, five staffers burst into her hospital room and began feverishly attending to her. She did not rouse during their skillful work.

Then the physician explained in a layperson's terms that my mother had experienced the pulmonary equivalent of a code blue. The hospital's monitoring equipment sent out the SOS, and the staff came running to assist her. The physician said, "At this juncture, you must decide. Your mother either needs to be put into the ICU or transferred to a palliative care unit."

Only because my mother had given me the gift of such unambiguous instructions and had done so repeatedly, I knew what decision I had to make to honor my mother's wishes. When I told the medical team that my mother only would want to go to palliative care, in an instant, I next found myself looking at five of the broadest smiles I had seen.

From their expertise, they knew it was pointless to put my mother in the ICU. Medical staff is accustomed to hearing family emotionally, though not rationally, indicate, "Do whatever you can!" when doing so is fruitless, painful, and robs the dying of a short time of peacefulness before their imminent death.

Despite the incredible abilities of modern medicine, my mother would have been made enormously uncomfortable despite the best efforts of the staff to mitigate her pain, some of which would have been caused by the invasive ministrations of an ICU hospital room. It would have hurt my mother, wasted Medicare resources, and violated my mother's wishes. I would have broken my promise to her and failed her while accomplishing no positive end for her whatsoever. It explained why five professionals were reflexively beaming at me in unison.

I did not even see it as my decision; my mother had made her decision. My task was to be the messenger for my mother's decision when she could no longer decide and speak for herself, which is precisely the purpose of a health-care POA. As my mother's attorney-in-fact or agent, she, as the principal, had delegated authority for me to act on her behalf, making medical decisions for her based on her instructions in the HPOA.

Only because my mother had been so clear and persistent, I felt no guilt in instructing the medical staff that my mother would prefer palliative care. I received the gift of knowing what to do and the gift of not having to fret or feel guilty over my instructions for my mom.

In a lengthy discussion with an ICU nurse and her husband, she explained her wishes if she was a patient in an ICU. Though she had seen successful cases who had recovered after extensive ICU stays, some lasting months, her wish for herself only, based on her experience and preference, was if she was making no progress after seven days of ICU care, her instructions to her husband were to discontinue her treatment.

The more clearly and frequently you communicate your wishes to your family, you help them enormously when they need to act. Please give them that gift through discussions where you make your preferences known, asking them to reflect to you what they heard that you want. You will likely feel better you did so, and you will reduce the size of their decision-making burden and particularly their need for unnecessary feelings of guilt over following your wishes. They will know what to do, which will please them as they honor you.

The Big Picture

You have a salient choice; now you can begin to do your work to get organized for your estate-related issues, which will save your family time, effort, confusion, aggravation, pain, and probably money. Alternatively, you can do nothing or little now and potentially leave a giant mess for your family after you die. We do not know the day or the hour.

I see your effort to become prepared for death as being a generous, prudent, caring gift to those you love. Your loving efforts include meeting with an attorney to have the appropriate legal documents drawn up for yourself and your family, getting organized with your statements and records, and communicating your overarching wishes to those you love. Your prep and their preparation can prove priceless in a crisis.

Decide who is on or off your team. Get a skilled attorney, investment adviser, tax adviser, insurance agent, and any other professionals needed to maximize the effectiveness of your preparation for yourself and those you love. Doing so will help to minimize the extra work of your family during a crisis. I hadn't met one person who said to me, "Michael, I wish I was less well prepared when my spouse died." I have had numerous clients be thankful that the extra time, guidance, and encouragement they received from me made their heavy burden lighter.

There's an inescapable truth. Either you will do the work while living, preferably while you are well, or someone will get stuck doing a tremendous amount of work when you are fighting a severe medical condition and sadly after you are gone. My viewpoint, which is a by-product of my work, teaching, and personal experience, is if someone you love is trying to settle the most uncomplicated estate, it is still a pain in the tail for them to do so even with the significant advantages of planning and organization. When I share this observation as I am teaching, I have a roomful of students vigorously nodding their heads in agreement.

While excellent preparation reduces the headaches of the personal representative, the successor trustee, and other family members, it does not eliminate them. Trust me that I am 100 percent accurate about this. I have experienced it myself and have experienced it vicariously through hundreds of individuals and their family' situations with which I have helped over more than thirty-five years.

In contrast, without preparation and the needed legal documents, it can instead be a chaotic nightmare, coming at precisely the worst moment, when people you love are beset with fear over the progression of a virulent disease and later wounded by the most profound grief.

With the best preparation, none of this is easy for the caregiver, who may wear multiple hats as the FPOA and MPOA agent, later as the executor, the successor trustee, to name only four possible formal roles. As difficult as it is for the well prepared, trust me when I say that it is magnitudes of difference worse for a family that is unprepared for severe illness and death.

I once had the spouse of a client frantically call me. Sadly, her husband had a massive heart attack, and he was in critical condition. She needed me to send a large amount of money to her home to meet current and future anticipated expenses. I noticed no FPOA on her husband's retirement account, so I explained if she could send me a copy of his durable financial power of attorney. Once it was reviewed and accepted by our mothership, my team could instruct the custodian to issue a check promptly. We didn't need the original document, just a copy of the FPOA, which she could have faxed or scanned to us quickly.

Her reply was heartbreaking. "Michael, I wanted him to go see an attorney as you recommended, but he wouldn't do it. We don't have anything we need." I then had to explain that as she was not an owner on any of his assets, the custodial firm and I were powerless to meet her request to distribute any of his funds. Meanwhile, he was in ICU and was not conscious, so he could not sign or instruct us to send his funds to him.

"Michael, what do I do?" "You will need to visit an attorney who may need to petition the court for access to your husband's funds."

Two months later, she was able to request funds, though not because the wheels of justice had raced forward. Her husband had died, and since she was his primary beneficiary, we could distribute to her any or all his retirement account funds (via the most undesirable reason to receive access to needed funds). While she waited with dwindling funds, you can readily empathize over how she felt.

While she was going through the worst event in her life as her husband was dying, she had this significant unneeded burden. The irony is they had plenty of assets as a couple but no essential legal documents to rapidly request and receive a needed distribution. Whether you prepare is your choice.

I respect if you are feeling ill that while battling a severe, even life-threatening, disease, you may not feel up to doing all the tasks needed to protect yourself and those you love. It will not help you to chide yourself over what you didn't previously tackle. I have met so many caregivers who pile on themselves needless guilt, feeling that they could have done more or performed their tasks better. We are back to the debilitating, "I should have, we ought to have, I wish I had done." Often, what I find is some of the most amazing caregivers I have been privileged to meet are the most self-critical. If you are too harsh and unrealistic when doing a self-appraisal, you will achieve nothing of worth except grading yourself unfairly.

Whatever your circumstances, list your needs or those of someone you love. It is vital to ask everyone you trust to pitch in. Break down each task, or preferably so you can rest and heal, have a loved one break down each task into small, manageable components. "Inch by inch, everything is a cinch" goes the aphorism. What looks like it is impossible to do can be done by you or someone you love or trust if the parts are made small enough.

So many people tell me, "Michael, I initially had no idea how difficult it was for Mom and Dad. They hid their challenges well. They said they didn't want to bother me because they know the demands on me raising my kids. I wish they had told me sooner." This reticence to explain their challenges and hardships is such typical parental behavior. My clients in their seventies, eighties, and nineties were shaped by their parents and grandparents who went through the unfathomable pain and arduousness of the Great Depression. Knowing how hard their economics of the Depression and the WWII era were on families, I ask my clients married forty-five, fifty-five, and sixty-five years what material support they received from their families was when they were newlyweds. They laugh as they look back on their humble beginnings, telling me, "Michael, all we had in our pockets as we married were the best wishes of our families." Others will say to me, "Michael, when we were kids, we did not realize that our family was poor since everyone around us had about the same as our family did. Then when we became adults, we realized that though somehow our parents made it through, they didn't have much."

Many of my clients, like their parents and grandparents before them, tended to learn not to complain about the adversities of life. They were unaccustomed to announcing their hardships. They believed it was their duty to just grin and bear it. If you are the caregiver, your loved one may not share with you some aspects of their challenges out of embarrassment as a result of how they were socialized and enculturated. They may withhold their deepest fears.

If you talk with your loved one seeking to elicit how they feel, mainly focusing on their fears, you may be able to help them unpack some of their worries while giving you more significant insights in the totality of their current concerns and experiences. A way to introduce discussions about emotions and fears that may help you broach the topic is to say something like, "Mom or Dad, I try to imagine if I were in your shoes what I may be feeling. Can you help me understand what it's like for you now? What thoughts and feelings can you share with me so I may be able to help you better?"

Many people tell me that there are just a few conversations with some loved ones that stand out to them years later as being so consequential as each bared their innermost thoughts, fears, and deepest longings. You do not control if your loved one chooses to be transparent. You will feel good you tried your best to create fertile conditions for the most profound sharing if they do open up as a result of your efforts, which can prove magical for everyone involved.

You can prepare well. It's worth it to you and those you love even if trouble doesn't find you or your family for many years as you will have the satisfaction of knowing you gave your family the labor of your love for their protection.

Finally, praise to all caregivers; your burdens are many. Your gifts of love, attention, support, and assistance are incomparable, and they will console you when you lose someone you love deeply. Every day of life, if we bring the attitude of gratitude, is a treasure beyond measure. Prepare! Enjoy! MCW.

INDEX